Thomas William White

Our English Homer

Or Shakespeare Historically Considered

Thomas William White

Our English Homer
Or Shakespeare Historically Considered

ISBN/EAN: 9783744642125

Printed in Europe, USA, Canada, Australia, Japan

Cover: Foto ©Thomas Meinert / pixelio.de

More available books at **www.hansebooks.com**

OUR ENGLISH HOMER;

OR,

SHAKESPEARE

HISTORICALLY CONSIDERED.

BY

THOMAS W. WHITE, M.A.

Μουσάων Ἑλικωνιάδων ἀρχώμεθ' ἀείδειν (*Hesiod's Theogony*, 1).

LONDON:

SAMPSON LOW, MARSTON & COMPANY,
LIMITED,

St. Dunstan's House,

FETTER LANE, FLEET STREET, E.C.

1892.

LONDON:
PRINTED BY WILLIAM CLOWES AND SONS, LIMITED,
STAMFORD STREET AND CHARING CROSS.

PREFACE.

THE prevalent notion that Shakespeare was a poet, who owed little or nothing to education and everything to original genius, is the opinion that was for many years entertained regarding Homer. And the opinion seems to have obtained among some, from the early days of the seventeenth century. Thus we have it on the authority of Nicholas Rowe that " In a conversation between Sir John Suckling, Sir William D'Avenant, Endymion Porter, Mr. Hales of Eton and Ben Jonson, Sir John Suckling, who was a professed admirer of Shakspeare, had undertaken his defence against Ben Jonson with some warmth. Mr. Hales, who had sat still for some time, told them that if Mr. Shakspeare had not read the ancients, he had likewise not stolen anything from them, and that if he would produce any one topick, finely treated by any one of them, he would undertake to shew

something upon the same subject at least as well
written by Shakspeare" ('Some Account of the
Life of William Shakspeare,' p. ix). And Dr.
Johnson writing in 1765 makes the assertion
that, "The greater part of his (Shakespeare's)
excellence was the product of his own genius.
He found the English stage in a state of the
utmost rudeness, no essays either in tragedy or
comedy had appeared from which it could be
discovered to what degree of delight either one
or the other might be carried." . . . . And he
adds, "Perhaps it would not be easy to find any
author, except Homer, who invented so much"
('Preface to the Plays,' pp. lv and lviii). But
the old fashioned idea of Homer, a blind beggar
unable to read or write, who, inspired by the
divine spirit within him, wandered through the
cities of Asiatic Greece chanting the epic which
delights the world, has long since been abandoned by classical scholars, so that unless
Shakespeare be the sole example, the history of
mankind affords no instance of a man without
education having produced a literary work of
the highest excellence. Yet that is what we
are required to believe in the case of Shakespeare. He is described by his contemporaries—

and nothing has transpired to contradict them
—as being without learning or art, and yet as
having produced works fit, as Ben Jonson says,
to compare with—

All that insolent Greece or haughty Rome
Sent forth, or that did from their ashes come.

Surely such a proposition must be strictly
proved before reasonable people can believe it;
surely the matter must always remain open to
doubt until it is proved. And to the few, who
trouble themselves with probabilities, it has been
for many years a doubtful question ; while some
have cut the knot by finding a more likely author
in our great philosopher, Francis Bacon. Meanwhile the patient labour of skilful investigators
has shown that certain well-known Elizabethan
dramatists were undoubtedly engaged in the
composition of the plays, and that all that could
be claimed either for Shakespeare or Bacon was
a final revision of so material a kind as would
constitute practical authorship.

Now at first sight it does not appear why
the discussion of this question should raise either
heat or acrimony. We are in possession of those

inimitable dramas ; and it can therefore matter
very little to us whether they were written by
one man or another.   Shakespeare has not, like
Homer, been deified.   His temples do not adorn
the land, and no vested interests seem to belong
to his worship.   When, however, we remember
how much learned criticism has been written on
the assumption that he is our divine bard, the
vested interest at once appears.   How can we
expect ingenious ladies and gentlemen to tolerate
a theory, which suggests the propriety of burning
their books.   I have, nevertheless, been driven
to the conclusion, that Shakespeare had nothing
to do with the composition of the plays ; that
Bacon began the series by writing ' Hamlet,' and
was afterwards employed to revise those which
Shakespeare bought of other playwrights.

I make no claim for the discovery of facts
before unknown.   Everything in that shape had
been already discovered, or at least suggested
before my time ; and all that remained to do,
was, to marshal the evidence and draw from it a
consistent conclusion.   In thus doing I have
aimed at producing a popular treatise, which will
place before the general public, the information
hitherto confined to specialists.   Every reader

will thus be able to form an opinion of his own,
if he disagrees with mine.

But, though I have gladly availed myself of
information wherever it was to be found, I have
been unable to make any use of Mr. Donnelly's
'Great Cryptogram.' I do not pretend there is
no cryptogram in Shakespeare's Plays; but I
am sure Mr. Donnelly errs in thinking he has
discovered one.

In dealing with the subject I have chosen
as my starting-point, Dr. Johnson's celebrated
" Preface." I have selected it in preference to
more modern criticisms, chiefly because, on it
our common opinion was originally founded, but
partly also because, in spite of some judicial
errors and much want of scholarship, it displays
a calm impartiality, which does not always
characterize modern critics.

The following are the editions of the principal
works consulted, and in many of the quotations
from which I have ventured to modernize the
old forms of spelling :—

I. 'Poetical Works of Samuel Daniel.' 1718.
II. Mallet's ' Life of Bacon,' Mallet's Works. 1759.
III. 'Romeo and Juliet,' by De Vega (English). 1770.

IV. Nicholls' 'Six Plays.' 1779.

 V. 'The Plays of William Shakspeare.' London,
    1803.

    N.B. To this edition is prefixed 'Rowe's Memoir
    of Shakspeare,'. and 'Dr. Johnson's Preface to
    the Plays,' 1765.

VI. Bacon's Works. 1819.

VII. Collier's 'History of English Dramatic Poetry,'
    1831.

VIII. Dyce's 'Robert Greene.' 1831.

IX. Riddle's 'Illustrations of Aristotle from the
    Dramatic Works of Shakespeare.' 1832.

 X. Wharton's 'History of English Poetry.' 1840.

XI. Collier's 'Shakespeare's Library.' 1848.

XII. Dyce's 'Marlowe.' 1850.

XIII. 'The Philosophy of Shakespeare's Plays Unfolded,'
    by Delia Bacon. 1857.

XIV. Lord Campbell's 'Shakespeare's Legal Acquire-
    ments.' 1859.

XV. Spedding's 'Life of Bacon.' 1861.

XVI. Hepworth Dixon's 'Personal History of Lord
    Bacon.' 1861.

XVII. 'The Authorship of Shakespeare,' by N. Holmes.
    1866.

XVIII. Gifford's 'Ben Jonson.' 1870.

XIX. 'Chapman's Plays.' 1874.

XX. Shakespeare Society's Publications, viz:
    Allusion Books, 1874—
        Greene's 'Groatsworth of Wit.'
        Chettle's 'Kind-heart's Dream.'
        Meres' 'Palladis Tamia.'
    Allusion Books, 1879—
        Ingleby's 'Centurie of Prayse.'

Series II., 1874—
    Daniel's ' Romeo and Juliet.'   Parallel : text
    of first and second quartos.
XXI. 'Shakespeare's Poems.'   1878.
XXII. Halliwell Phillips's 'Outlines of the Life of Shake-
speare.'   1886.

T. W. W.

CONTENTS.

APPENDICES.

OUR ENGLISH HOMER;

OR,

SHAKESPEARE HISTORICALLY CONSIDERED.

——◦◦◦——

CHAPTER I.

STATE OF ENGLISH LITERATURE WHEN SHAKESPEARE APPEARED.

Classical learning—Euphuism—Tone of thought—The New
Philosophy—Poor scholars.

THE re-enlightenment of Europe, after the long
reign of ignorance in the Middle Ages, was still
in an early stage when Shakespeare's plays made
their appearance. It had begun with the invention of printing in the middle of the 15th
century; and it was greatly accelerated by
the overthrow of the Lower Empire a century
later (1543), when the treasures of Greek literature, especially the works of Aristotle, were
carried into the West by the fugitives from
Constantinople. But it was not until the
Reformation had set men's minds free, that any

real progress was made in enlightening the people of England. And, even then, it was no more than a dawning. Thus Dr. Johnson justly says that—

> The English nation, in the time of Shakespeare, was yet struggling to emerge from barbarity. The philology of Italy had been transplanted hither in the reign of Henry VIII., and the learned languages had been successfully cultivated by Lily, Linacre and More, by Pole, Cheke and Gardiner, and afterwards by Smith, Clerke, Haddon and Ascham. Greek was now taught to boys in the principal schools ; and those who united elegance with learning, read with great diligence the Italian and Spanish poets. But literature was yet confined to professed scholars or to men and women of high rank. The public was gross and dark ; and to be able to read and write was an accomplishment still valued for its rarity.   (*Preface to Shakespeare's Plays, pp.* xlix–l.)

But the literature then in vogue aimed only at reproducing the learning of the ancients, as it had come down to modern times. There was no notion of bettering the instruction. So each writer chose his favourite author and dressed him in English, endeavouring on other occasions to make him the model of his own style. Thus Richard Carew, writing in 1595, says—

> Whatever grace any other language carrieth is lively represented in ours. Will you have Plato's vein ? Read Sir Thomas Smith ; the Ionics ? Sir Thomas More ; Cicero's ? Ascham ; Varro ? Chaucer ; Demosthenes ? Sir

John Clarke. Will you read Virgil? Take the Earl of
Surrey; Catullus? Shakespeare and Marlowe's fragment;
Ovid? Daniel; Lucan? Spenser; Martial? Sir John
Davies and others. Will you have all in all for prose and
verse? Take the miracle of our age, Sir Philip Sidney.

(Excellence of the English Tongue.)

The English language was, nevertheless, still
barbarous and uncouth. It was not merely
deficient in elegance, it had adopted neither just
principles in etymology nor in syntax. Its
poetry, refined by the restrictions of metre, was,
without doubt, excellent; but its prose, in which
no such restraint existed, remained, like an un-
weeded garden, overrun by a rank luxuriance
which almost obscured the flowers of knowledge
and judgment. And it is remarkable that, in this
respect, the age of Plautus and the age of Shakespeare were alike; for Plautus, like Shakespeare,
wrote at a time when there was no literary language. Yet Varro could say, if the Muses spoke
Latin, they would choose the tongue of Plautus;
and we, perhaps, might say the same of Shakespeare. If, however, we compare the style of the
Umbrian bard with the fragments of Philemo, and
that of the Elizabethan poet with Aristotle, we
shall see that both the one and the other were
greatly indebted to antiquity for the beauties of

B 2

their style. And this leads us to another characteristic of Elizabethan literature.

In 1580, John Lily published ' Euphues ; or, the Anatomy of Wit,' and in 1581 'Euphues and his England.' The style of composition thus inaugurated was distinguished by its constant use of antithesis and simile, a style that had been adopted two thousand years before by Aristotle. And there can be no doubt those two figures greatly increase the force of rhetoric— the first intensifying a proposition by contrast, while the latter reveals it by illustration. The vice of Lily's system was that, in trying to be always antithetical, he often became ridiculous, and that his crowd of similes frequently obscured the meaning they were intended to elucidate. The fashion he had set, its faults notwithstanding, was speedily domiciled at Court; and conceit and frivolity, taking possession of it, converted it into a jargon, which is cleverly burlesqued in Osric's speeches to Hamlet (v. 2). The following extracts from ' Euphues ' will, however, afford a fair specimen.

Antithesis.

Thou *weepest* for the death of thy daughter ; and I *laugh* at the folly of the father; for greater vanity is there in the mind of the mourner than bitterness in the death of the deceased. But she was *amiable;* but yet *sinful.* But she was young and might have *lived;* but she was mortal and must have died. Aye; but her *youth* made thee often *merry;* aye; but thine *age* should make thee *wise.*

Simile.

There are three things which cause perfection in a man —nature, reason, use. Reason I call discipline; use exercise. If any of those *branches* want, certainly the *tree* of virtue must needs wither.

A less pedantic example may be quoted from Greene, one of Lily's disciples.

The brother of this diabolical atheism is *dead* and never in his *life* had the felicity he aimed at; but as he *began* in craft, *lived* in fear and *died* in despair. This *murderer of many brethren* had his conscience seared *like Cain;* this *betrayer* of Him that gave His life for him, inherited the portion of *Judas;* this *apostate* perished as ill as Julian.

(*Groatsworth of Wit.*)

The prevailing tone of thought, meanwhile, strongly tinctured as it was with the maxims of pagan philosophy, was still in most cases subject to the prejudices of mediæval superstition. Some, adopting the teaching of Lucretius in his *De rerum naturâ,* became atheists; but the generality held to the Mosaic cosmogony and the system of Tycho Brahé, believing also in witchcraft, hobgoblins, omens and dreams. So far

as philosophy and science existed at all, they
were comprised within the four corners of
Aristotle's teaching. He, it was fondly believed,
had found out everything that could be discovered, and that prolonged inquiry was nothing
less than an audacious attempt to pry into
secrets which the God of Nature had chosen to
conceal. And yet alchemy and other kinds of
natural magic had many professors and more
dupes. The correct opinion of course was that
they were not sciences, but black arts, whose
instigator was the devil; but in certain cases
they changed their hue, and became the *media* of
piety and religion.

But while the authorities in learning were
contenting themselves with the crumbs of
knowledge, which had reached them through the
lapse of twenty centuries, a New Philosophy was
being inaugurated, which was destined to hurl
Aristotle from his pedestal, and change the
whole current of educated thought. A gay
young lawyer, one Francis Bacon by name, who
had been born and bred in the Court of Elizabeth,
was making the most astonishing of proposals,
with an audacity which was absolutely sinful.
He not only proposed to treat the magicians

and astrologers as impostors, he was for includ-
ing the divine Stagirite in the same category,
alleging that the only difference between them
was, that the one was "a folly speaking in
whispers ; the other, a folly which cried aloud."
He therefore proposed to cast the teaching of
antiquity aside, and commence the pursuit of
knowledge by studying nature in experiment.
And he promised as boldly as any magician
could. "Now," he seemed to say, "we have
faint reflections in a mirror, which the magicians
tell us is truth ; but then we shall see it face to
face ; and those, who have hitherto deluded us
with the phantasmagoria of error, will be able to
delude us no more." Can we not fancy how
all the learned doctors shook their heads ? Can
we not picture the Master of Trinity turning
pale with rage, as he listened to what his former
pupil had said? That wily ecclesiastic must
have foreseen that, if young Bacon's scheme were
adopted, the long reign of priestcraft must come
to an end, and the people become their own gods,
knowing good and evil. Is it surprising that
with all the advantages of genius and of learning,
in spite of his high connections, Bacon, who
panted to devote his life to the study of nature,

was denied the necessary provision? But so it was. The father of modern philosophy was compelled to spend his early manhood in the drudgery of the law; and the new philosophy slept as long as Elizabeth occupied the throne.*

One other important feature of the time remains to be noted. This was the rise of a class of poor scholars who, before the Reformation, would have gained their living as priests, but who now sought to live by literature. They seem to have fancied that as the Reformation had set the minds of the people free, they might earn their crust by distributing to them the wealth of the temple of knowledge. And so they might have done, if the Reformation had really been what they imagined it to be, but it was far otherwise. It had severed the nation from Rome and opened the people's eyes to its grosser impostures; but it had not overthrown the power of the clergy. That remained almost as great under the English sovereign as it had been under the Roman Pope. They still ruled in the church and the universities, to which all

---

* The invention of logarithms, however, by John Napier, Baron Merchiston, was a contribution to the study of astronomy, which was found to be subsequently of great importance.

the rewards of scholarship were confined ; and scholars, though never so learned, still required to be fed. Some few wealthy Protestants took individuals under their protection, and paid for the publication of their literary compositions ; while others engaged them as tutors, and paid them the wages of menial servants. But the bulk of them had to depend on the booksellers and the players—the former as rapacious as booksellers always have been ; the latter as extortionate as ignorance and greed could make them. And the circumstances of the times served to increase the evil. The reading public and the playgoers kept no proportion with the number of scholars which the universities were every year turning out to seek a living where they could find it. How their numbers reduced the value of their work must be self-evident. How their struggle to live was attended by want, and vice, and misery, requires no one to explain. As a matter of fact, the life of scholarship became synonymous with a life of despair. Take an illustration from one of two plays lately discovered (1887), in Hearne's Collection in the Bodleian ; viz., 'The Pilgrimage to Parnassus,' acted during the Christmas of 1598 at St. John's

College, Cambridge, and 'The Return from
Parnassus,' performed at the same place in 1599.
The first describes the university career of two
youths, Studioso and Philomusus, and also
introduces Ingenioso, a disappointed author;
but the second gives us the story of their
subsequent battle with the world. And what is
its upshot? Philomusus settles down as a
sexton, while Studioso becomes tutor in a
family, where he has to eat with the servants
and work in the fields during harvest. As for
Ingenioso, he sinks into the dependant of one
Gullio, who employs him to write books, which
he publishes as his own. But as we shall,
hereafter, have occasion to refer particularly to
some of those poor scholars, we will here give a
short sketch of their lives.

George Peele was born in Devonshire about
the year 1553. He was educated at Broadgates
Hall, now Pembroke College, Oxford, and took
his A.M. in 1579. He was a popular poet eight
years before we hear anything of William
Shakespeare. In 1584 he was conductor of the
Court pageants, and his charming pastoral
comedy, 'The Arraignment of Paris,' was performed before Queen Elizabeth. Five years

later (1589) he was engaged at the Blackfriars theatre. But in 1592 we have it on record, that he was "driven to extreme shifts," and threatened with the loss of such support as the stage .had afforded him (*Groatsworth of Wit*). He died in 1598 of a loathsome disease (*Palladis Tamia*) before he had attained his forty-sixth year.

Thomas Lodge was born in Lincolnshire of respectable parents. He entered Trinity College, Oxford, as a servitor in 1574, and took his A.B. in 1575. Soon after he commenced the experiment of living by literature, becoming a poet, dramatist, and novelist. In 1585 he joined Cavendish in his voyage round the world,* and on his return, in 1588, entered himself at Lincoln's Inn. In 1589 he terminated his

* In the 'Supplement of the Introduction to the Shakespeare Allusion Books' (p. xxxvii) it is stated that Cavendish left Plymouth in August 1591; but the writer is evidently confounding the expedition of Cavendish with that of Lancaster and Rimer, who merely went to the East Indies, as Cavendish .had completed his circumnavigation in 1588, after having been absent three years, while Lancaster and Rimer began their voyage in 1591 (Wade's 'British Hist.,' London, 1839, pp. 150, 151). But what conclusively settles the question is, that Lodge's novel of 'Rosalind,' which he says he composed to relieve the tedium of his long voyage, was first published in 1590 (*Allibone's 'Dict. of Eng. Lit.'*).

connection with the stage and devoted himself
to more serious literature. And we have it,
under his own hand, that he was thoroughly
ashamed of the time he had thus wasted. In
the last stanza of his poem of 'Glaucus and
Scylla' (1589), he says :

> And then by oath he bound me,
> To write no more of *that whence shame doth grow*,
> Or tie my pen to penny knaves' delight,
> But live with fame and so for fame to write.

He subsequently studied medicine at Avignon,
and finally settled in London as a physician,
where he died of the plague in 1625, aged
sixty-nine.

George Chapman was born in 1557, at or near
Hitchin, in Hertfordshire. There seems to be
some doubt about his university career ; but he
was probably a scholar of Trinity College,
Oxford. He was famous among his contemporaries as a classical scholar, and has the honour
of being the first who translated Homer into
English. He also tried to live by literature,
and wrote plays, which were brought out by
Henslowe and Alleyne, the rival theatrical
proprietors to Burbage and Shakespeare. Though
a man of careful and temperate habits, he was

no stranger to the penury which attended the life of scholarship, especially during the earlier part of his career. But he was generously patronized by Francis Bacon and Prince Henry during his later years, and died in 1634 at the age of seventy-seven.

Thomas Nash was born at Lowestoft, in 1558, and though educated at St. John's College, Cambridge, was presumably the son of poor parents. That he attributed his wretchedness to having been educated above his station, may be gathered from his 'Pierce Penniless':

> Ah! worthless wit, to train me to this woe,
> Deceitful wits that nourish discontent,
> Ill thrive the folly that bewitched me so.
> Vain thoughts! adieu! for now I will repent.
> And *yet my wants* persuade me to proceed;
> *For none take pity of a scholar's need.*
> Forgive me, God, although I curse my birth,
> And ban the air wherein I breathe a wretch,
> Since misery hath daunted all my mirth,
> And I am quite undone through promise-breach.
> Ah! friends,—no friends that then ungentle frown
> When changing fortune casts us headlong down.
>
> (*Pierce Penniless*, 1592.)

And there can be no doubt that his life was miserable in the extreme. Misery in fact is the burden of this, his best-known work. Thus he says:

Having spent many years in studying how to live and lived a long time without money—having tired my youth with folly and surfeited my mind with vanity, I began at length to look back to repentance. I sat up late and rose early, contended with cold and conversed with scarcity ; *for* (but ?) all my labours turned to loss. My vulgar muse was despised and neglected, my pains not regarded or slightly rewarded, and I, myself, in prime of my best wit, laid open to poverty.   (*Idem.*)

For a short time, during 1592–3, he was patronized by Archbishop Whitgift, who had been Master of Trinity, when he was a student at its neighbour John's ; but the patronage soon ceased. The Archbishop, who had been attracted by the spirited satire on the Puritans in 'Martin Marprelate,' probably wished to enlist him as a servant of the Church ; but, as we have said, it was the idiosyncrasy of all the poor scholars to reject that servitude, so Nash was once more thrown upon his own resources ; while the Archbishop joined with the Bishop of London in procuring an order from the Privy Council for the destruction of his pamphlets wherever they were found. No doubt the poor folks at home did what they could for their unhappy son; but Lowestoft, in his day, was not a place whence much help could be expected. It must have been little better than a fishing-village, though the curing of herrings had already been established there. But this reminds us of the story told by Gabriel Harvey, that Robert Greene, another of the poor scholars, whose biography will appear later, had not died of want, but of a surfeit of pickled herrings and Rhenish wine. No doubt a supper of such fare did take place, at which both Greene and Nash were present; and if Greene were in a famishing condition, he would be very likely to take too much. Be that as it may, the herrings and the Rhenish, too,* were, in all probability, a present from Lowestoft, which Nash, with true Bohemian generosity, shared with his unfortunate friend. Nash died in the year 1600, when little past forty.

Samuel Daniel, the son of a music-master, was born at Taunton, in 1562, and was educated, probably by the aid of the Earl of Pembroke, at Magdalen Hall, Oxford, which he entered as a

---

* The principal, if not the only, export trade from Lowestoft was to Amsterdam, Rotterdam and Hamburg. We may, therefore, fairly assume that Rhenish wine constantly found its way to it.

commoner in 1579. After three years' residence
he left the University and was engaged by the
Earl as tutor to his son William Herbert, whom
he accompanied to Italy. He was similarly employed in the family of the Earl of Cumberland,
his pupil being Anne Clifford, afterwards famous
as the Countess of Pembroke. But at Oxford he
had become a worshipper of the muses, and he
remained more a professional author than a
schoolmaster, and figures most conspicuously as
a poet, dramatist and historian. He always seems
to have enjoyed the patronage of the great;
and, on the death of Edmund Spenser in 1599,
he was made poet-laureate. He may never have
sounded those deeper depths of penury, in which
so many poor scholars were engulfed; but he
was always a poor man, though no one better
deserved a peaceful competency. Thus, Fuller
says that—

His father was a master of music; and his harmonious
mind made an impression on the genius of his son, who
proved an exquisite poet. . . .

He was a pious man, who abhorred all kinds of
profaneness. (*Worthies of England—Somerset.*)

But he was destined to experience not only
the pinching of poverty, but the hostility of

enemies. And his letter to the Earl of Devonshire, formerly Lord Mountjoy, gives significant
evidence of the fact, while it shows his own
manly spirit. Early in the reign of James, his
tragedy of 'Philotas' had been presented to the
Privy Council as a treasonable work; and he
had been summoned before the lords to answer
the charge. In doing so he had appealed to the
Earl's knowledge of him and the tragedy in
question—an appeal that had greatly offended
his lordship. Hence the letter, which is as
follows:

My Lord,
      Understanding your Honour is displeased with
me, it hath more shaken my heart than I did think any
fortune could have done; in respect I have not deserved it,
nor done or spoken anything, in this matter of 'Philotas,'
unworthy of you or *me*. And now, having satisfied my
Lord Cranbourne, I crave to unburthen me of this
imputation, with your honour. And it is the last visit I
will ever make. And, therefore, I beseech you to understand all the great error I have committed. First I told
the lords, I had writ three acts of this tragedy the
Christmas before my Lord Essex's troubles, as divers in
the city could witness. I said the Master of the Revels
had perused it. I said I had read some parts of it to your
Honour. And this I said, having none else of power to
grace me, now in Court and hoping that you, out of your
knowledge of books and favour of letters and me, might

C

answer them, there was nothing in it disagreeing, nor
anything—as I protest there is not—but of the universal
notions of ambition and envy, the perpetual argument of
books and tragedies. I did not say you encouraged me
unto the presenting of it. If I should, I had been a
villain; for that when I showed it to your honour, I was
not resolved to have had it acted; *nor should it have been,
had not my necessities overmastered me.* And, therefore, I
beseech you, let not an Earl of Devonshire overthrow what
a Lord Mountjoy hath done who hath done me good; and
I have done him honour. The world must and shall know
my innocence, whilst I have a pen to show it. For that
I know I shall live *inter historiam temporis,* as well as
greater men, I must not be such an object unto myself
as to neglect my reputation. And having been known
throughout all England for my virtue, I will not leave a
stain of villainy upon my name, whatsoever else might
'scape me unfortunately, through my indiscretion and
misunderstanding of the time. Wherein, good my Lord,
mistake not my heart, that hath been and is a sincere
honourer of you and seeks you now for no other end, but
to clear itself and to be held as I am, though I never come
near you more.

Your honour's poor follower and faithful servant,

SAMUEL DANIEL.

(*Calendar of State Papers—Domestic Series—Reign of
Elizabeth,* 1602–1603—*London,* 1857.)

But though Daniel had been able to disprove
the charge of disloyalty, his enemies did not
relax their malignant efforts. Ben Jonson,

who, compared with him, was only a mechanical
and uncouth rhymster, was put forward to
supersede and did practically supersede him in
the laureateship, and lost no opportunity of
depreciating him. Thus he told Sir William
Drummond that Daniel was a good, honest man,
but no poet; and that only he (Jonson) and
Chapman knew how to write a court masque
(Jonson's Works, iii. 490). And Daniel's own
words show that, so early as 1607, he had lost
much of his popularity. Thus, in the dedication
to Prince Henry prefixed to 'Philotas,' 1607, we
read :

> And I, although among the latter train,
>   And least of all that sung unto this land,
> Have borne my part, though in an humble strain,
>   And pleased the gentler that did understand ;
> And never had my harmless pen at all
>   Distained with any loose immodesty,
> Nor ever noted to be touched with gall
>   To aggravate the worst man's infamy,
> But still have done the fairest offices
>   To virtue and the time. Yet nought prevails,
> And all our labours are without success ;
>   For either favour or our virtue fails.
> *And, therefore, since I have outlived the date*
>   *Of former grace, acceptance and delight,*
> I would my lines, late-born beyond the fate
>   Of her (Elizabeth's) spent line, had never come to
>   light.

So had I not been taxed for wishing well,
　Nor now mistaken by the censuring stage,
Nor in my name and reputation fell,
　Which I esteem more than what all the age
Or earth can give.　But years have done this wrong
To make me write too much and live too long.

For some years Daniel nevertheless withstood the secret hostility which had been raised against him ; but in 1615 he left London for ever, and retired to a small farm, probably provided by the Countess of Pembroke, at Beckington, near Phillips Norton, in his native county ; where he died four years after, at the early age of fifty-seven.　His old pupil, after she had become a widow, erected a monument to him in Beckington church.

Christopher Marlowe, the greatest genius, perhaps, of the whole fraternity, was the son of a shoemaker at Canterbury, and was born there in 1565.　He was educated first at the King's School in that city and afterwards at Benet's College, Cambridge, which he entered as a pensioner in 1580, taking the degree of A.B. in 1583 and A.M. in 1587.　He seems to have commenced dramatic composition while he was still at the university, the first part of his tragedy of ' Tamburlain ' having been produced at the Curtain in 1587. Either then, or later he became one of the actors at the Curtain, and continued in that employment until incapacitated by an accident, in which he broke his leg. We next hear of him (1592) not only as writing plays for Shakespeare's company, but as participating in their debauchery, until their " loose lives " had made religion loathsome " in his cars." And it is a matter of notoriety that he lived and died a professed atheist. It is, however, remarkable that all the plays which bear his name were acted, not at the Blackfriars theatre, with which Shakespeare was connected, but at the Curtain, with which he had nothing to do. Marlowe's career as a littérateur was eminently successful ; and we hear nothing in his case, either of poverty or persecution. He was fatally wounded during an affray in a brothel at Deptford, and died some days after, before he had attained his twenty-ninth year (June 1593).

Now these biographies, as a whole, show we have not exaggerated the facts in our general description of the poor scholars ; but the last two may convince us that their misfortunes were not entirely due to natural causes. A

powerful conspiracy seems to have existed
against them.   And its *modus operandi* was
marked by the deepest subtlety.   If the literate
were viciously inclined, it allowed him full
means of indulgence ; if his inclination were to
virtue, no effort was spared to counteract his
exertions.   It was undoubtedly a clever scheme ;
and the conspirators, as they watched the game,
might always have been saying, " Heads, we
win ; tails, you lose."   For, if Daniel's experience shows how difficult they made it for a
virtuous man to succeed, Marlowe's shows how
easy they made it for a vicious one to fail.

CHAPTER II.

STATE OF THE DRAMA.

'Gorboduc'—Dramatists of the Period.

THE popular drama which had now superseded the Miracle Plays of the clergy, was an imitation of classic models, and was for the most part clothed in decasyllabic blank verse. That form of poetry had been introduced by the Earl of Surrey in the reign of Henry VIII., he having borrowed it from the Italian poets. The following may be taken as a specimen of his translation of the second and fourth books of Virgil :—

> Reginam thalamo cunctantem ad limina, primi
> Pœnorum exspectant, &c.   (*Æn*. iv. 133.)

> At the threshold of her chamber door,
> The Carthage lords did on the queen (Dido) attend.
> Her trampling steed, with gold and purple trapt,
> Chawing the foaming bit, there fiercely stood.
> Then issued she awaited, with great train,
> Clad in a coat of Tyre embraded rich.
> Her quiver hung behind her back, her tress
> Knotted in gold, her purple vesture eke
> Buttoned with gold.
>   (*Wharton's Hist. Eng. Poetry*, iii. 36.)

But the popular drama, as we have said, began in an imitation of the Grecian stage. Thus, so early as 1561, Thomas Sackville, Lord Buckhurst, afterwards Earl of Dorset, produced his 'Gorboduc,' formed on the lines of Greek tragedy. It had a regular chorus, but its episodes were divided into five acts. It, too, was written in decasyllabic blank verse. Great improvements had, however, been made in the English language, during the forty-eight years which had elapsed since Surrey's translation of Virgil (1513), as the following declamation on civil war will show :—

> And thou, O Britain, whilome in renown,
> Whilome in wealth and fame shalt thus be torn,
> Dismembered thus, and thus be rent in twain,
> Thus wasted and defaced, spoiled and destroyed.
> These be the fruits your civil war will bring,
> Hereto it comes when kings will not consent
> To grave advice, but follow wilful will.
> This is the end when, in fond princes' hearts,
> Flattery prevails and sage rede hath no place.
> These are the plagues when murder is the mean
> To make new heirs unto the royal crown.
> Thus wreak the gods when that the mother's wrath
> Nought but the blood of her own child can 'suage.
> These mischiefs spring when rebels will arise
> To work revenge and judge their prince's fact.
> This, this ensues when noble men do fail

In loyal truth, *and subjects* will be kings.
And this doth grow when, lo ! unto the prince,
Whom death, or sudden hap of life bereaves,
No certain heir remains.

The plot, which is as regular and consistent as that of Greek tragedy, pretends that Gorboduc, a king of the ancient Britons, having divided the kingdom between his sons Ferrex and Porrex, abdicates and retires, with his wife, into private life. But the brothers are not content with their respective patrimonies. They rush into war against each other, and Porrex being vanquished is put to death. Thereupon his mother murders Ferrex. Then the people rising kill both her and Gorboduc (*Wharton*, iii. 40).

This play was never, so far as we know, represented in any theatre nor by any company of professional actors, its first performance being by the students of the Inner Temple, of which Lord Buckhurst was a bencher ; but it properly stands at the head of the Elizabethan drama.

About the same time or soon afterwards appeared the ' Cambyses ' of Dr. Preston and Kydd's ' Hieronimo.' Both pieces are entered on the Stationers' Register for printing in 1564, and both took their places on the stage.

After these three we have a long array of dramatists, many of whom had produced plays before we hear anything of Shakespeare. Terris, Watson, the Earl of Oxford, Dr. Gager, Rowley, Edwards, Gascoyne, Heywood, Peele, John Lily, the Euphuist, Lodge, Chapman, Nash, Robert Greene, Henrie Chettle, Munday, Samuel Daniel, Drayton, Middleton, Marston, Porter, Wilson, Weaver, Hathway, and Marlowe. And some of the early pieces kept the stage and were popular favourites long after the Shakespearian dramas had been brought out. Thus, from the " funeral elegy on the death of the famous actor, Richard Burbage, who died on Saturday, in Lent, the 13th of March, 1618," we learn that he was as famous in Kydd's ' Hieronimo,' as in ' Hamlet,' ' Lear,' or ' Othello.'

> He's gone, and with him what a world are dead
> Which he revived, to be revived so
> No more—young Hamlet, old Hieronimo,
> Kind Lear, the grieved Moor, and more beside
> Which lived in him have now for ever died.
> <div align="right">(<i>Centurie of Prayse</i>, <i>p</i>. 131.)</div>

Thus Preston's ' Cambyses ' is referred to as a work of importance by Falstaff (Hen. IV., Pt. 1, ii. 4), and a speech from Peele's ' Tale of Troy '

is introduced with commendation into 'Hamlet'
('Hamlet,' ii. 2); while Ben Jonson, in his
praise of Shakespeare prefixed to the first folio,
alludes to Kydd and Lily's comedy and
Marlowe's tragedy.

But the English stage seems to have been
indebted to other than classic models. Isaac
D'Israeli first, in his 'Curiosities of English
Literature,' and then Payne Collier, in his
'History of English Dramatic Poetry,' have
pointed out that an intercourse existed between
the Italian and English theatre as early as 1578,
when an Italian *commediante* was in London
with his company. And the former writer, in
his article on Massinger, Milton, and the Italian
comedy, calling attention to the Platts (Plots)
discovered at Dulwich College, suggests that
they were precisely similar to the *scenarii* or
written directions for the Italian extemporal
comedies. And he thence argues that such
entertainments were not uncommon on the
English stage, supporting his proposition by the
evidence of Gabriel Harvey and Francis Meres,
who speak of the extemporal wit of Tarleton
and other actors. And here, of course, our
minds revert to Hamlet's advice to the players,

and we not unnaturally conclude, from his reproof of those clowns, who say more than is set down for them, that the habit of extemporising remained, even when the piece had been fully written.*

Again, we may not unfairly infer that Italian pantomimic acting was known in England before Shakespeare's time. True, it may be, that John Rich, the contemporary of Garrick, who played under the name of Lun, was the first to introduce the dumb-show we call pantomime; but the Italian mimics were not dumb. And, as D'Israeli suggests, their *capitan*, a reproduction of the *Miles Gloriosus* of Plautus, may have been the type of our Pistols and Bobadils; as the inferior characters may have given the idea of our witty or quasi-witty clowns.

* In the Italian extemporal comedy a succession of scenes were inscribed on the *scenario*, the dialogue being left to the impromptu invention of the performers. D'Israeli gives the following description of the plot of the *Seven Deadly Sins* found at Dulwich. It is written, he says, in two columns on a pasteboard about fifteen inches high, and nine in breadth. "A tent being placed on the stage for Henry the Sixth, he in it asleep. To him the lieutenant and a *pursuivant* (R. Cowley—Jo. Duke) and one warder (R. Pallant). To them Pride, Gluttony, Wrath and Covetousness, at one door, at another door Envy, Sloth, and Lechery. The three put back the four, and so *exeunt*. Henry awaking, enter a keeper (J. Sincler); to him a servant (T. Belt); to him Lidgate; then Envy passeth over the stage. Lidgate speaks."

We are not forgetting those Court Masques, which formed so striking a contrast in their magnificence to the squalid representations on the professional stage. They formed no part of the popular drama, but were amusements confined to the Court and the great families; and they cannot be included in the true dramatic art. They were classical allegories, attempting no delineation of character in action, their representatives speaking without passion, and only being distinguishable by their dress and ornaments. See Francis Bacon's 'Essay on Masques.'

From what has thus been shown we conclude that, though still in its infancy, the English drama had commenced its career twenty-eight years before Shakespeare appeared.

CHAPTER III.

SHAKESPEARE'S WORKS.

The Plays—Their Characteristics.

THERE is a similarity between the works of
Homer and Shakespeare which must strike every
student.   As the former contains the great mas-
terpieces, the 'Iliad' and 'Odyssey,' and the less
meritorious 'Batrachomyomachia,' Hymns and
Epigrams, so the latter has his inimitable plays,
and the inferior poems of 'Venus and Adonis,' the
'Rape of Lucrece,' Sonnets, &c.; and as Homer
is best known to us as the author of the 'Iliad'
and 'Odyssey,' so Shakespeare, in his plays, is
"familiar in our mouths as household words."
But the plays, so far as we know, did not create
any great popular sensation.   Indeed, from all we
hear, Kydd's 'Hieronimo,' Preston's 'Cambyses,'
and Chapman's 'Bussy d'Ambois' were as great
favourites with the town as 'Hamlet' or 'Romeo
and Juliet.'   It may have been that the new

drama was above the tastes of the general public ;
or that, on its first introduction, the pieces
composing it wore a ruder shape than they
subsequently attained. As they now appear,
however, there can be no doubt that, with some
exceptions, they are immeasurably superior to
their contemporaries. Their characters are more
distinct and natural, and their action more
animated, while their declamation is enriched
with such striking thoughts and beautiful
expressions as we find nowhere else.

Their characteristics may be placed under the
heads of STRUCTURAL, LITERARY, and QUALITA-
TIVE.

Under the head of STRUCTURAL the first trait
which strikes us is *verisimilitude.* The plots, it
must be allowed, constantly violate probability ;
but the characters and incidents are always
consistent with experience. As Dr. Johnson
says, " The event represented will not happen ;
but if it were possible, its effects would probably
be such as are assigned." Thus Caliban is a
creature unknown to humanity, but he acts and
speaks as such a being would do, if it did exist.
Then Shakespeare is almost alone among contemporaries and successors in frequently rejecting love

as the motive of his drama. Thus love is entirely absent from 'Macbeth,' 'Henry IV.,' 'Julius Cæsar,' 'Coriolanus,' 'Timon of Athens,' 'Richard II.' and 'King John ;' while its presence is only an incumbrance in the 'Merchant of Venice,' 'Lear,' and 'A Midsummer Night's Dream.' Then the blending of comedy with tragedy is a peculiarity of his drama, which has found no imitators and very few apologists. And lastly, the want of moral purpose is peculiarly his own. Dr. Johnson says, "He sacrifices virtue to convenience, and is much more careful to please than instruct. From his writings, indeed, a system of social duty may be selected, for he that thinks reasonably must think morally ; but his precepts and axioms drop casually from him ; he makes no just distribution of good or evil" (p. xxxviii). He writes, in fact, as immoral men generally act, praising virtue with the mouth, but practising vice in the life. Not one of his plots brings the virtuous out in triumph. Lear seems intended as a reproof of filial ingratitude, and Hamlet as a commendation of filial piety ; but Regan and Goneril suffer no worse fate than Cordelia, while Hamlet is involved in the same destruction as the King and Queen. The Merchant of

Venice meanwhile justifies the ingratitude of Jessica. It is her *praise* that she leagues with her father's enemies, and that she robs as well as deserts him; and we are only required to laugh when told of the unhappy man's distraction; for it is an excellent joke to hear that all the boys in Venice do follow him, crying, "His stones, his ducats, and his daughter."

The LITERARY characteristics of the plays are, without doubt, their most important feature. Apart from them, and viewed only as dramas, our critic was certainly right when he said: "He has scenes of undoubted and perpetual excellence, but perhaps not one play which, if it were now exhibited as the work of a contemporary writer, would be heard to the conclusion" (p. lx). It is the literary beauties which always have and always must command our applause. And yet beside those beauties, and often obscuring them, we find what can only be appropriately described as *fustian*. We shall not stop now to consider how the incongruous conjunction occurred. It did occur, and we have it before our eyes whenever we take up our Shakespeare. Dr. Johnson, without attempting to search for reasons, admits the fact in the following striking remark: "Other

D

poets," he says, "display cabinets of precious
rarities minutely finished, wrought into shape
and polished into brightness. Shakespeare opens
a mine which contains gold and diamonds in
unexhaustible plenty, though clouded by incrus-
tations, debased by impurities, and mingled
with a mass of meaner minerals" (p. liii). And
those baser products, which we call his fustian,
have at least three varieties. There is *bombast*
and *laborious declamation* where ease and
simplicity might be expected of any average
writer. As our critic says, " In narration he
affects a disproportionate pomp of diction and a
wearisome train of circumlocution, and tells the
incident imperfectly in many words which might
have been more plainly delivered in few" (p. xl).
Of this the instances are so numerous that we
may well leave the reader to select one from
almost any of the tragedies or histories—from
any one, in fact, if we omit ' Hamlet,' ' Romeo
and Juliet,' and ' Othello.' But the next form,
which appears, we think, in ' Hamlet' alone, and
which may be described as *Absurd Amplifica-*
tion, will be at once recognised in the following passage, where we have placed the fustian
in italics :—

This heavy-headed revel, east and west,
Makes us traduc'd and tax'd of other nations :
They clepe us, drunkards, and with swinish phrase
Soil our addition ; and indeed it takes
From our achievements, tho' perform'd at height,
The pith and marrow—
> *of our attribute.*
> *So oft it chances in particular men,*
> *That for some vicious mole of nature in them,*
> *As, in their birth (wherein they are not guilty*
> *Since nature cannot choose his origin),*
> *By the o'er-growth of some complexion,*
> *Oft breaking down the pales and forts of reason ;*
> *Or by some habit, that too much o'er-leavens*
> *The form of plausive manners ;—that these men,—*
> *Carrying, I say, the stamp of one defect ;*
> *Being nature's livery, or fortune's star,—*
> *Their virtues else (be they as pure as grace,*
> *As infinite as man may undergo)*
> *Shall, in the general censure, take corruption*
> *From that particular fault.*
>   The dram of base
Doth all the noble substance often dout,
To his own scandal.

(*Ham.* I. 4.)

Now the passage, read without the lines in
italics, is clear sense harmoniously expressed ;
while with them it is a farrago of discordant
nonsense.

The third form which the fustian takes is
that of ridiculous jests, quibbles, and conceits,

and which become all the more striking from
contrast with the better humour we are constantly meeting. No doubt much of what we
call wit loses its salt by effluxion of time,
because it so often depends on passing fashions
and changing opinions; but true wit, like true
wisdom, is for all time. The fustian, however,
to which we are objecting seems to have been
offensive to men of taste even in Shakespeare's
own time. They called it trunk-hose wit, such
as could only please the vulgar. Thus, in the
address prefixed to the first folio of Beaumont
and Fletcher's plays, we read :

> Shakspeare was early up and went so drest
> As for those dawning hours he knew was best ;
> But, when the sun shone forth, these two thought fit
> To wear just robes and leave off *trunk-hose* wit.

But on this point Dr. Johnson's opinion
must be the opinion of every judicious critic.

"The admirers of this great poet," he says,
"have most reason to complain, when he approaches nearest to his highest excellence. . . . He
is not long soft and pathetick without some idle
conceit or contemptible equivocation. . . . A
quibble is to Shakespeare what luminous vapours

are to the traveller. . . . It is sure to lead him out
of his way and sure to engulf him in the mire.
. . . . Whatever be the dignity or profundity of
his disquisitions . . . . let but a quibble spring
up before him, and he leaves his work unfinished"
(p. xli). And, to pass over the coarse jests and
contemptible quibbles, what shall we say to a
conceit like the following, occurring as it does in
one of the most pathetic scenes of 'Romeo and
Juliet'?

Friar. Come, is the bride ready to go to church?
Cap. Ready to go, but never to return.
  O son, the night before thy wedding day
  Hath death lain with thy bride. See, there she lies,
  Flower as she was, deflowered by him.   (IV. 5.)

But when all is said that can be said respecting
the fustian, beauties enough remain to justify
the esteem our bard commands. His language
—and in his day the English tongue was still
unsettled—displays an excellence that can only
be approached by copying it. He seems, in fact,
to have transferred our vernacular from the
common speech of men to the language of the
gods; and, in that respect, he not only surpasses
us moderns, he has no equal among his contemporaries. Ben Jonson, Beaumont and Fletcher,

Massinger, or even Dekker may have excelled him as a dramatist; but, in comparison with his, their language is poor and weak. Yet, when we come to analyse it, we find that, though it may be a more refined euphuism than theirs, it is euphuism nevertheless, expressing its thoughts by means of antithesis and simile. Thus, under the former figure, we have such passages as—

> And yet for aught I see, they are as sick who surfeit with too much, as they that starve with nothing.
> (*Merchant of Venice*, I. 2.)

and—

> I like not fair terms and a villain's mind.
> (*King John*, I. 1.)

while under the latter we have—

> Now is the winter of our discontent
> Made glorious summer by this sun of York.
> (*Richard III.*, I. 1.)

and—

> Care keeps his watch in every old man's eye;
> And where care lodges sleep will never lie.
> (*Romeo and Juliet*, II. 3.)

It contains, however, an element which theirs usually wants : it is rich in proverbial philosophy. Where else do we find passages like—

> The sleeping and the dead
> Are but as pictures. 'Tis the eye of childhood
> That fears a painted devil.   (*Macbeth*, II. 2.)

and—

> Time hath, my lord, a wallet at his back,
> Wherein he puts alms for oblivion.
>
>   (*Troilus and Cressida, III.* 3.)

This may exhaust the purely literary characteristics, but the language of the plays is pregnant with QUALITATIVE elements that distinguish it from all others. Other writers of the period draw their illustrations from what was then thought the only fount of poetic description, the pagan mythology. Shakespeare, on the other hand, has recourse to natural philosophy, astronomy, medical science, and English jurisprudence. This is so obvious that we have treatises on his knowledge of each. Thus we have 'The Philosophy of Shakespeare's Plays Unfolded,' by Delia Bacon, London, 1857; 'Shakespeare's Medical Knowledge,' by W. Stearns, M.D., New York, 1865; 'A Medico-chirurgical Commentary on Shakespeare,' by W. Wadd, *Quarterly Journal of Science*, 1829; 'Shakespeare a Lawyer,' by W. L. Rushton, Liverpool, 1857; and 'Shakespeare's Legal

Acquirements,' by John Lord Campbell, London, 1859.

But, though Shakespeare avoids the then fashionable habit of classical illustration, his plays reveal a vast amount of classical erudition and an intimate acquaintance with Spanish and Italian literature—subjects we shall discuss farther in considering the originals of his dramas.

CHAPTER IV.

ORIGINALIA LATINA.

Plautus—Terence—Livy.

THE subject of foreign literature in Shakespeare's plays has brought us naturally to the question of originality. We do not pretend that any literary work can be absolutely original; knowledge and art being, from the nature of things, matters of evolution. We only propose, therefore, to enquire whether the plays are original, within the limits of possibility—that is, whether the mind of the author, having been schooled in the literature of the past, had applied itself to the task of composition, without further reference to it; or whether he had simply copied from it, limiting his own efforts to such changes as would produce a colourable alteration. And, as regards *Latin literature*, our conclusion is that he has copied. Two of the comedies are mere adaptations from Plautus; while speeches, characters and incidents are taken bodily from Terence and Plautus.*

Thus the 'Comedy of Errors' is an adaptation of the 'Menæchmi.' This will be seen from a slight sketch of the Roman play.

The plot, as described in the prologue, supposes that—

A certain merchant of Syracuse had twin sons, so much alike that even their mother could not distinguish one from the other. When the children were seven years old, their father took one of them with him on a voyage to Tarentum. There, as it happened, great crowds had assembled to witness the public games, and among them the child was lost. He was found by a merchant from Epidamnus, who took him

---

* Of late years it seems to have become the fashion for persons to undertake the exposition of Elizabethan literature, who are entirely unacquainted with the Latin dramatists, regardless of the fact that Elizabethan writers were all forming themselves on classical models. A very curious illustration of the result may be found in the Mermaid Edition of Dekker's plays, London, 1887. Thus in the 'Shoemaker's Holiday' (I. i., p. 12) we have an amazing note on the following speech of Eyre to his wife:

"Away with your pishery-pashery, your *pols* and your *edepols*."

The editor explains that "*pols* and *edepols* is apparently one of Eyre's *improvised phrases*, referring to his wife's trick of repeating herself!" *Pol* or *edepol* is, however, a Roman oath, meaning *by Pollux*, and, like *ecastor*, *by Castor*, was in common use on the Roman stage.

to that city. The father was so much distressed by the loss of the boy, that he died at Tarentum a few days afterwards. A messenger having reported these things to the grandfather of the children, he changed the name of the child that was at home to Menæchmus, the name borne by him who was lost.

The Epidamnian merchant, meanwhile, who had great wealth, but no children, adopted Menæchmus, got him a rich wife, and dying made him his heir. And, in those comfortable circumstances, the young man remained an inhabitant of Epidamnus.

But now the twin brother of Syracuse sets out in search of the one that was lost, and in the course of his journeying arrived with his servant at Epidamnus.

The characters put in action are Menæchmus of Epidamnus, his wife, her father, Peniculus his parasite, Erotium a courtesan of Epidamnus, Cylindrus her cook, her female servant, a physician of Epidamnus, Menæchmus of Syracuse and his servant, Messenio. The stage shows, on one side, the house of Menæchmus of Epidamnus, and, on the other, the house of Erotium; and the drama, of course, passes in front of them.

The piece opens with a humorous soliloquy by Peniculus, who has come, as usual, to feast at the expense of his patron, but Menæchmus has other views. His rich wife has no charms for him, and he is resolved to dine with Erotium. When, therefore, he makes his appearance, the courtesan is summoned and directed to prepare a repast for the three, and he gives her a robe he had just stolen from his wife. The parasite and he then repair to the forum until the dinner is ready.

The second act introduces us to Menæchmus of Syracuse and his servant, who have just arrived at Epidamnus. Erotium, who issues from her house at this juncture, naturally mistakes this twin brother for her friend Menæchmus of Epidamnus. She treats his disclaimer of acquaintance as a jest, and insists on his going in to the dinner she has prepared. After some parleying he consents; while his servant, taking charge of his purse, returns to their inn.

The third act brings back Peniculus, who, having lost sight of his patron in the forum, is under the idea that he has purposely given him the slip and is gone alone to enjoy himself with the courtesan. While he is bemoaning the loss of his dinner, Menæchmus of Syracuse comes from the courtesan's house. He wears a garland, like one who has already feasted, and is greatly elated at the good fortune that has so unexpectedly befallen him, for he has not only feasted at the expense of Erotium, she has given him the robe her real lover had presented to her, that he may take it to the embroiderer. Peniculus of course begins to upbraid him; while he, as much of course, denies all knowledge of him. This is too much for the parasite's patience; and he goes off to tell the wife how she has been spoiled to gratify Erotium. But fate has not yet finished loading the traveller with unexpected and inexplicable favours. No sooner has the parasite left him than Erotium sends her servant with the gold bracelet which he is said to have given her on some former occasion, in order that he may take it to the goldsmith and have an ounce of gold added to it. With these spoils he determines to gain the shelter of his inn, and, throwing off the garland to facilitate his escape, leaves the stage.

In the fourth act, while the wife and the parasite are conferring, her husband, who has

been detained by clients in the forum, makes his
appearance, and is about to enter the courtesan's
house for the purpose of dining, when his wife
stops him ; and such a scene ensues as any one
may imagine. To his great surprise he finds
that the parasite has betrayed him in regard to
what had happened ; while he appears to have
invented circumstances in which he had never
been placed. He, however, makes a lame
defence of what is true, by alleging that he has
only lent the robe ; and, as his wife's anxiety is
confined pretty much to her wardrobe, she orders
him to bring it back, if he wishes to enter
her house again ; and so she leaves him. But
now the confusion becomes worse confounded.
Having called Erotium out of her house, he begs
her to return the robe, promising to give her one
of double the value. "But I gave it to you to
take to the embroiderer," she cries, "and also
that bracelet." It takes but a short time to put
the courtesan in a rage. "You want your gifts
back again. Keep them and enjoy them, you
or your wife, and stuff them into your eyes.
After to-day you never enter my house again."
And she goes in and bangs the door after her.
Thus shut out both by wife and mistress, and

hungry withal, he retreats to take counsel with his friends.

The fifth act is opened by the wife of Menæchmus of Epidamnus and Menæchmus of Syracuse. She has come out to await the return of her husband; he is searching for his servant, Messenio, and still carries the robe and the bracelet.

"I acted very foolishly," he says, "when I entrusted Messenio with my purse. He has soaked himself in some brothel, I suppose."

"There he is," says the wife, "and he has got the robe. Now I shall receive this man as he deserves." And she begins: "Are you not ashamed to appear before me with those things in your hand?"

Of course he denies all knowledge of her, and chaffs her pleasantly, when she says she will rather live a widow than submit to such treatment; nor is he alarmed when she sends a servant to fetch her father. He doesn't know him from Calchus—as we should say, from Adam; and he confesses a like ignorance of her grandfather. But the father comes, and the moralizing, with which he opens his part, reminds us forcibly of the fatuous wisdom of Polonius.

But his sagacity is at last upset. Menæchmus sticks to it that he knows neither him nor his daughter, and asserts that he has never yet set foot in her house. At this point the wife fancies he is mad.

"Do you not see," she cries, "that his eyes are growing green? that a green colour is over-spreading his face and temples?"

On which Menæchmus concludes that he cannot do better than pretend to be out of his mind, in order to drive them away, and begins to rave in the most approved fashion, declaring that Apollo has ordered him to burn out her eyes and break every bone in the old man's skin. She accordingly takes refuge in the house, while her father goes for a physician. Menæchmus, thus freed from them, retreats to his ship.

Then the old man returns with the physician; and, while they are talking together, Menæchmus of Epidamnus arrives. The scene which follows is very amusing. Though he, of course, betrays no signs of mental aberration, and answers the ridiculous questions of the physician as any other sane man might do, he loses patience at last and wishes him at the devil.

Qui te Jupiter diique omnes percontator perdiunt!

"Now indeed the man begins to be mad,"
cries the medical sage. "From those words
take heed." "Yes," replies the father dryly,
"but less from what he says now, than from
what he said a while ago. Then he called his
wife a mad dog." The end of it is that both
agree the man is mad. The father therefore
goes to fetch the town-beadles to carry the
maniac to the physician's house, where he is to
be treated with hellebore; while the unhappy
Menæchmus sits down at his own door.

Then Messenio comes to fetch his master from
the courtesan's house, and is followed by the
father and the beadles. He, of course, mistakes
Menæchmus of Epidamnus for him, and, when
the beadles attempt to drag him away, he beats
them off. Menæchmus fancies he must be mad
when his deliverer insists that he is his servant,
and petitions for his freedom. Messenio, however, is positive, and runs off to the tavern
to fetch the purse. Menæchmus of Syracuse
meanwhile is still in search of his servant, and
thus it happens that, while Menæchmus of
Epidamnus is waiting outside his house,
Messenio and Menæchmus of Syracuse successively arrive.

E

The dénouement follows naturally, and so the play comes to an end.

Now here we have not only a fairly reasonable plot and a drama composed of probable and effective incidents, but we have more. The *dramatis personæ* are all sufficiently characteristic, the parasite, the wife, the father-in-law, and the servant of Menæchmus of Syracuse being strongly marked individualities; while the dialogue is natural and brilliant, and strictly subservient to the business of the piece. There is not a superfluous incident, not a character too many, nor a word too much.

Yet the Shakespearian drama, formed from it, is the reverse of all that. It is a mere parody, vulgar, tedious and complicated almost beyond understanding. Like a tyro, who cannot resist the temptation to redundancy, the author not only puts the prologue into action, he goes to another play, the 'Amphitryo,' and borrows from it the idea of twin-servants, heedless of the fact that the plot of 'Amphitryo' required such an addition, while the fable of the Menæchmi does not. Then, though his stage is crowded with persons—he has sixteen besides mere attendants, against the eight employed by Plautus—there is not a character among them. Indeed, he entirely omits the father-in-law and the parasite, who are so effective in the original. But it is not only evident that the author was incapable of grasping the beauties of the Umbrian bard, we are inclined to fancy that he could not translate him; and that he makes Pinch a *conjurer*, because he constructed

Abiit socerus; abiit medicus. Nunc solus sum (V., v. 54)

as—

The sorcerer, the physician is gone. Now I am alone.

We have been thus particular in describing the Menæchmi because the 'Comedy of Errors' is such a contemptible parody of it.*

The 'Tempest' is another adaptation of Plautus. It is founded on the " Rudens," which may be thus described :—

The scene is laid on the sea-shore of Cyrenaica, the morning after a storm. On the right at some distance is seen the city of Cyrene ; on

---

* The finest adaptation from the Roman stage is undoubtedly ' The School for Scandal,' taken from the ' Adelphi' of Terence. It transcends as much as 'The Comedy of Errors' falls below its model.

the left, near at hand, is a temple of Venus and a cottage. During the prologue, a boat, containing two girls, is observed struggling with the waves in the distance. After a time, they succeed in landing on the stage. Both are the property of Labrax, a slave-dealer at Cyrene ; but one, Palæstra, is a free-born Athenian, who had been stolen in her infancy and sold. She, of course, is very beautiful, and an Athenian named Pleusidippus, having seen her at Cyrene, had fallen in love with her and agreed with Labrax to buy her. The slave-dealer, however, thinking he might make a better market of her elsewhere, had embarked with her and her companion for Sicily, and had been wrecked off the coast. The girls, after some opposition from the priestess, because they are not in white robes and have brought no offering for the goddess, find refuge in the temple.

Dæmones, the owner of the cottage, an Athenian whose daughter had been stolen in her childhood, and who, having left Athens, is living in retirement in the neighbourhood, now comes to superintend the repair of the cottage, which has been damaged by the storm.

Next Labrax appears on the scene. He, too,

has escaped the fury of the waves, though he has lost his wallet, containing all his money and a case of jewels and toys, which had been taken with Palæstra, when she was kidnapped. Hearing that his slaves have escaped, and that they are in the temple, he goes and drags them thence by force. He is, however, met by Trachalio, the servant of Pleusidippus, who is searching for Labrax and the fair Palæstra. Trachalio immediately applies at the cottage for assistance, and Dæmones and his slaves rescue the girls, and he takes them under his own protection. Then Labrax by the order of Pleusidippus, who opportunely arrives, is led off to the judge, to answer for his former breach of contract and his later act of sacrilege.

At this point a considerable interval of time is supposed to elapse.

The drama is resumed by Gripus, one of Dæmones' slaves. He has been fishing; and, though he has caught no fish, he has pulled up a wallet, which he deems from its weight to be full of money; and he immediately begins to say what great things he will do with his wealth as soon as he has purchased his freedom. But Trachalio has been watching him all the while,

and now comes forward, claiming to go halves in
the spoil. After a due amount of quarrelling,
Gripus, who knows nothing of Trachalio, nor of
the events that had formerly occurred in that
place, proposes that they shall apply to the
master of the cottage to arbitrate between them,
thinking that his master will be sure to decide
in his favour. Trachalio agrees, and Dæmones
proceeds to open the wallet. It not only
contains the money of Labrax, but the things
that had belonged to Palæstra ; and among the
latter he finds two toys, one inscribed with his
name and the other with that of his wife. This
convinces him that Palæstra is his long-lost
daughter, a free-born Athenian, and as such
worthy to be the wife of her lover, Pleusidippus.
Poor Gripus, it is almost needless to say, does not
realize the magnificent future—he had fancied
he might even found a new empire—that he had
anticipated. His master certainly applies some
of the money to the purchase of his freedom ;
but he also uses another part to enfranchise the
companion of Palæstra. The destination of the
residue may be easily conceived.

Though the 'Tempest' does not keep close to
its original, it is free from the faults which

disfigure the 'Comedy of Errors.' There is no
attempt to act the prologue. Prospero relates it
to Miranda, as they sit together after the storm,
and thus puts the audience in possession of what
is necessary to be known. Then the character
of Prospero (Dæmones), of Miranda (Palæstra),
and of Caliban (Gripus) are decided improvements on the original. There is also abundant
evidence that Plautus was thoroughly understood and appreciated by the author.

The 'Winter's Tale' probably explains why
Shakespeare was called the English Terence in
'The Scourge of.Folly,' 1611 (C. of P. p. 94).

The 'Andria' of Terence, on which it is
founded, supposes that a certain Athenian merchant, named Phania, has been wrecked on the
coast of Andros, along with his reputed daughter, Glycerie, then an infant. He takes up
his residence there, but after a while dies.
Glycerie, who is thus left unprotected, is brought
up by a native with his own daughter, Chrysis.
At his death the two girls emigrate to Athens.
There Chrysis becomes a courtesan, while Glycerie is taken by Pamphilus, a young Athenian,
who has fallen in love with her and wishes
to make her his wife. His father, Simo, how-

ever, regarding her as a stranger, and as such
incapable of contracting marriage with an
Athenian citizen, wishes him to marry Philumena, the daughter of his friend Chremes, a
brother of the deceased Phania. But Philumena
is beloved by Charines, the friend of Pamphilus, and the drama is chiefly occupied by the
consequent troubles of the lovers. At last Crito
of Andros, a friend of Chremes, arrives at
Athens and explains that Glyceric is not an
Andrian, but the daughter of the deceased
Phania. But now Chremes informs them that
his brother Phania had no child, and that
Glycerie must be his own daughter. During
the late wars, he explains, he had fled from
Athens, leaving his infant daughter in the
charge of Phania, who had promised to follow
him with the little girl; and that it must
have been while attempting to follow him that
he had been wrecked at Andros. Glycerie and
Philumena are therefore sisters; and so all
ends happily.

As the reader will perceive, the ' Winter's
Tale ' takes little more than the idea from
Terence ; and if Autolycus had not borne such a
family likeness to Davus, the roguish servant in

Terence, no one, perhaps, would have thought of connecting the two plays. Thus, of the twenty-five characters in Shakespeare, we can only identify three with those of the 'Andria'; viz., Florizel with Pamphilus, the old shepherd with Crito, and Perdita with Glycerie. But Autolycus (αὐτόλυκος) could not be ignored. He is not only a very wolf, he is one of the most amusing rogues who ever preyed on the simple and credulous.

To the above we may add 'Cymbeline,' which is little more than a dramatised version of the story told by Livy of Tarquinius Superbus (Liv. I. 57).

Of the speeches taken from the Roman drama, we may cite that of Romeo concerning the apothecary, copied from the 'Mercator.'

Cur ego vivo ? Cur non morior ? Quid mihi est in vitâ boni ?
Certum 'st ibo ad medicum atque ibi me toxico morti dabo.
(Merc. II. 4.)

> Well, Juliet, I will lie with thee to-night.
> Let's see for means. . . .
> I do remember an apothecary,
> And hereabouts he dwells, etc.   (<i>R. & J.</i> V. 1.)*

---

* 'Romeo and Juliet' was no doubt in its inception an adaptation of the 'Mercator,' as 'Othello' was of the 'Amphitryo'; but it is certain in the one case, and highly probable in the other, that Shakespeare was indebted for them to the Spanish drama. We have therefore included them both under Spanish originals.

Then we have the very words used by Hamlet, in the scene with his mother, taken from Plautus' 'Amphitryo.'

> What have I done that thou darest wag thy tongue
> In noise so rude against me?
>   Such an act
> That blurs the grace and blush of modesty?
>
> *   *   *   *   *
>
>   But go not to my uncle's bed.
> *Assume a virtue if you have it not.*   (*Ham.* III. 4.)
>
> *Quid ego fui qua istæc propter dicta dicantur mihi?*
> *Tute edictas facta tua. . . .*
> *Saltem tute si pudoris egeas, sumas mutuum.*
>   (*Amph.* II. 2.)

So also the violence of Laërtes, when he breaks upon the king after his father's death, is a reproduction of Amphitryo's fury when Jupiter leaves him with the intention of visiting Alcmena.

> How came he dead? I'll not be juggled with.
> To hell, allegiance! Vows, to the blackest devil!
> Conscience and grace, to the profoundest pit!
> *I dare damnation.* . . . . only I'll be revenged.
>   (*Ham.* IV. 5.)
>
> Certum 'st introrumpam in ædibus ubi quemque hominem
>   adspexero,
> Sive ancillam, sive servum, sive uxorem, sive adulterum,
> Sive patrem, sive avum videbo obtruncabo in ædibus—
> *Neque me Jupiter, neque dii annis id prohibebunt.*
>   (*Amph.* IV. 3.)

In 'King Lear,' too, one of the most touching scenes, that between Cordelia and her father when he is awaking from his long sleep, is but a paraphrase of the scene in Plautus' 'Amphitryo,' between Bromia and Amphitryo, when the latter is recovering from the effects of the thunderbolt.

Cor. How does my royal lord? How fares your majesty?
Lear. You do me wrong, *to take me out o' the grave.*
    ＊   ＊   ＊   ＊   ＊   ＊

Cor.   Oh! look upon me, sir,
    And hold your hands in benediction o'er me.
    ＊   ＊   ＊   ＊   ＊   ＊

Lear.   Pray do not mock me.
    I am a very foolish, fond, old man
    Four-score and upward; and, to deal plainly,
    I fear I am not in my perfect mind.
                       (*King Lear*, IV. 7.)

Brom. Surge—
Amph.   Interii—
Brom.   Cedo manum—
Amph.   Quis me tenet?
Brom. Tua Bromia, ancilla—
Amph.   Totus timeo; ita me increpuit Jupiter,
    Nec secus est quam si *ab Acherunte veniam.*
                       (*Amph.* V. 1.) ＊

But it is not only in speeches that Shakespeare

＊ In 'King Lear,' also, two passages of great power are taken from fragments of Pacuvius, that describing the storm from the fragment of 'Dulorestes,' and that on fortune from the fragment of 'Hermione.'

has reproduced the Latin drama. All the humorous characters of this comedy are culled from that source, some being reproductions of individuals, others amalgamations of several persons. Thus Dame Quickly reproduces the Cleærita, Doll Tearsheet, the Philenum, and Bardolph, the Libanus of the 'Asinaria'; while Polonius is a combination of the Senex of the 'Menæchmi' and the Demea of the 'Adelphi.' Falstaff, as we see in Fuller's 'Worthies of England,' was likened to Thraso, in the 'Eunuchus' of Terence; but his impudence and cowardice, his burlesque moralizing and irresistible humour, his selfishness, cunning and want of principle prove his relationship to all the swash-bucklers, parasites and servants, whose portraits have been painted by Plautus and Terence.

CHAPTER V.

ORIGINALIA GRÆCA.

Æschylus—Sophocles—Homer—Plutarch—Aristotle.

THAT Shakespeare's plays owed something to Greek literature was perfectly understood before the grave had closed over their proprietor. Thus we have a distinct allusion to the fact in Anthon's ' Philosophical Satires,' published in 1616, where we read :

> Or why are women grown so mad,
> That their immodest feet like planets gad,
> With such a regular motion to base plays ;
> Where all the deadly sins keep holidays ?
> There shall they see the vices of old times,
> Orestes' incest (parricide ?), Cleopatra's crimes.

The slip in writing (if it be not a printer's error), " incest " for " parricide," does not affect our argument, the passage being a sufficiently obvious allusion to ' Hamlet ' and ' Antony and Cleopatra ' as imitations of the ' Electra ' of Sophocles and the life of Marc Antony by Plutarch. But those are not the only pieces taken from the Greek. 'Macbeth' is nothing but an English adaptation of the 'Agamemnon' of Æschylus. As, however, both the 'Agamemnon' and the 'Electra' are founded on the same Greek fable, it will render our subject more complete to refer to it.

We find it first in Homer; but as additions are made to it both by Pindar and the tragedians, it is not easy to judge what were the precise terms of the original legend with which Homer dealt. Modified as it has been, it reads as follows :—

The Grecian fleet, destined for the siege of Troy, having assembled at Aulis, was detained there by contrary winds, which the soothsayers declared to be due to the wrath of Artemis, whom Agamemnon had offended at some previous period. Thereupon they advised that his daughter Iphigeneia should be offered as a propitiatory sacrifice to the incensed goddess.* She was accordingly fetched from home, and was already bound and laid on the altar, when a cloud concealed her from sight. On its clearing

---

* Homer does not mention Iphigeneia, nor does she appear in any writer previous to Æschylus.

away a goat, or, according to Ovid, a hind, was found in her place, which was sacrificed in her stead.* The maiden was nevertheless lost to her family, Artemis having carried her away to Taurica Chersonesus (Crimea), where she became the priestess of her temple. Clytæmnestra, the wife of Agamemnon, had meanwhile formed an illicit connection with Ægisthus, the cousin of Agamemnon, who had been left in charge of the Kingdom of Argos, during the king's absence at the siege of Troy. On her husband's return she receives him with ostentatious demonstration of respect, offers a sacrifice, spreads a banquet, and is presumably ready to receive him to her couch. But all this outward parade of affection is only intended to throw him off his guard. As he leaves his bath, she presents him with a tunic, the sleeves of which have been sewn up; and, while he is entangled in it, she kills him with an axe. She had intended to kill his young son, Orestes, before his return; but the child had been rescued by his sister, Electra, who had sent him to his uncle, the King of Phocis. Thence, when grown up, he returns, having been com-

---

* Æschylus knows nothing of this act of deliverance, leaving it in doubt whether she was killed or not.

manded by the Oracle to avenge his father, and kills both his mother and her paramour. The rest of the fable, which relates how he was tormented by the Furies on account of his matricide, how he was purified from his crime, and how he finally recovered his sister, Iphigeneia, from Taurica Chersonesus, has nothing to do with our subject.

The plot of 'Agamemnon,' if plot it can be called, is confined to the assassination of that hero ; but the drama, constructed on that single incident, is by no means the least effective of the tragedies extant.

The scene is laid before the palace of Agamemnon, the *dramatos prosōpa* consisting of six persons and the chorus,* viz., Agamemnon, Ægisthus, Clytæmnestra, Cassandra, a watchman (φύλαξ), and Tulthybios, the herald (κηρύξ). The chorus is composed of old men (χόρος γερόντων), too old, as it appears from their own words, to have followed Agamemnon to the siege of Troy.

I. When the piece opens, the watchman is

---

* It is commonly said that Æschylus increased the number of actors from one to two. It would, perhaps, be more correct to say that he introduced dialogue by putting two *speaking* actors on the stage at one time, exclusive of the chorus. This is evident from the number of performers (six) in the tragedy before us.

discovered on a tower of the palace, who informs
the audience that he is set there to give notice
of the appearance of the beacon-fires which are
to announce the fall of Troy. Then he perceives
the first flash, and goes off to tell his mistress.
As he disappears the chorus enters. They tell
of the expedition that had left Argos ten years
before, and refer to the omen of misfortune
which attended it, and the unhappy fate of
Iphigeneia. Then Clytæmnestra enters, attended
by a procession of torch-bearers, and informs the
chorus that the fires now blazing on the hills
declare that the Grecian arms have been crowned
with success. Again, the chorus speak of the
omens with apprehension, and assert that the too
great success of mortals will often call down the
thunderbolt of Zeus, &c. :

πόθῳ δ' ὑπερποντίας
φάσμα δόξει δόμων ἀνάσσειν.* (404.)

II. The next episode introduces the herald
sent by Agamemnon to his wife, Clytæmnestra's
hypocritical professions of delight, and the
moralizing of the chorus, who, in spite of what

---

* " By (his) desire for her, (who is) over the sea (ὑπερ-ποντίας), a
ghost will seem to be queen of (his) home."

F

they have previously said, now assert that
justice directs everything ·to its destined end.*
Then Agamemnon appears in his chariot, accompanied by Cassandra, one of the daughters of
Priam, who has fallen to his share in a division
of the spoils of Troy, and a train of soldiers
bearing trophies.

This Cassandra is the great character of the
tragedy, and her declamation is, perhaps, the
very finest to be found in Æschylus. She
is a prophetess, though destined never to be
believed; and she now comes, bearing in her
hand the prophetic staff, and having her temples
bound with fillets. At the same time Clytæmnestra enters, attended by a troup of maidens,
bearing purple carpets, which she bids them lay
down, that Agamemnon may walk over them
into the palace. He objects that such arrogance
would be offensive to the gods, and only
consents to her urgent request after he has had
his buskins taken off. She and he then enter

* Professor Jebb, in an interesting article on Greek public
opinion, observes that the dramatic chorus is always made to represent it. In this case they do so most completely, now giving
way to popular superstition, when misfortune seems to lower, then
reverting to reason, as the prospect appears to brighten; and such is
always the custom of the vulgar herd.

the palace, leaving Cassandra, for whom he has bespoken a kind reception, still seated in the chariot.

III. The next scene is devoted chiefly to Cassandra. Clytæmnestra, who has returned from the palace, having ordered her to leave the chariot and commence her duties as a slave in the house, retires from the stage, leaving her alone with the chorus. The prophetess then alights, but, instead of entering the house, she takes the stage and bursts into a strain of lamentation, which gives us the finest declamation in the tragedy; while a vision of horrors already perpetrated, and of others yet to come, seems to pass before her. She describes the house to which she has been brought as shambles, and points, in confirmation, to the murdered children of Thyestes, murdered in that place long years before, when Atreus was King of Argos; and apostrophizing the Furies, who appear to her hovering over the blood-stained abode, she bids them complete their work. She sees the murder of Agamemnon as if it were taking place before her, crying out that a fell heifer is entangling the noble bull in her robes and goring him with her horns.

Then she reverts to her own unhappy fate,—
torn from a happy home to be butchered by a
monster; and addressing her native river, gives
us the type of the most pathetic speech in
' Macbeth ':

> ἰὼ Σκαμάνδρου πάτριον ποτόν ·
> τότε μὲν ἀμφὶ σὰς ἀϊόνας τάλαιν'
> ἠνυτόμαν τροφαῖς ·
> νῦν δ' ἀμφὶ Κωκυτόν τε κἀχερουσίους
> ὄχθους ἔοικα θεσπιῳδήσειν τάχα.   (1127.)

> Ah me ! Scamandros, native stream beloved,
> On thy fair banks I grew a happy maid ;
> But now beside the shores of Acheron
> And black Cocytos will my prophetic voice
> Too soon be heard.

reproduced, we think, by Macbeth, when he is
contemplating the approach of his fate :

> My way of life
> Is fall'n into the sear and yellow leaf ;
> And that which should accompany old age,
> As honour, love, obedience, troops of friends,
> I must not look to have.   (V. 3.)

IV. But now, recalling the bitter fact that no
one has ever believed her, she breaks her staff
and tears off her fillets ; and it is while thus

divested of prophetic insignia that her last vision takes place—the coming of Orestes, the avenger destined to bring Clytæmnestra to a bloody end. After that she essays to enter the palace, but starts back, averring that the place smells of blood, though as yet no slaughter has been effected. And then comes the last pathetic speech, which concludes her part:

ἰὼ βρότεια πράγματ᾽ · εὐτυχοῦντα μὲν
σκιά τις ἂν τρέψειεν · εἰ δὲ δυστυχῆ,
βολαῖς ὑγρώσσων σπόγγος ὤλεσεν γραφήν,

(1298.)

Alas! this mortal life! If prosperous,
'Tis but *a shadow;* but, if unfortunate,
With rapid strokes a weltering sponge wipes out
Th' entire picture, &c.

And this, as every one will see, is the model of Macbeth's soliloquy when told that his wife is dead:

Out! out! brief candle!
Life's but a *walking shadow*—a poor player
That struts and frets his hour upon the stage
And then is heard no more. (V. 5).

V. The last episode introduces us, of course, to the catastrophe. Agamemnon is heard crying out, as his wife attacks him; and the doors of the palace being thrown open, Clytæmnestra is discovered with the bloody axe in her hand, while the dead bodies of Agamemnon and Cassandra lie at her feet. And, in answer to the chorus, she justifies her deed as an act of vengeance due to her daughter Iphigeneia, and declares that she glories in the blood with which she is besmeared.

Such is the tragedy of 'Agamemnon'—a tragedy intended to illustrate the pagan doctrine of destiny. And it is not difficult to see how 'Macbeth' was formed from it. The author, feeling he could not tell a Christian audience that murders were the result of destiny, made ambition the motive. Clytæmnestra naturally suggested a murderess, and Thyestes a husband and conspirator; while Agamemnon was the proper victim; but there the δράματος προσῶπα seemed to fail him. Cassandra, a righteous prophetess under heaven's ban, was like nobody in the Christian world; the watchman and herald were only supernumeraries, and the chorus suggested no kind of individuality. But then came the happy inspiration of placing Cassandra on the stage, in the only

form sanctioned by popular sentiment, that is,
as a witch. Now witches at that time were not
usually young and beautiful, like Priam's
daughter ; but they had always been burnt
on the distinct understanding that they were
prophetesses ; and that was enough for him.
But he is not content with a prophetess.
Destiny is so constantly mentioned in his model
that he thinks it desirable to include it among his
characters ; and he goes to Hesiod's ' Theogony '
for information. There he first reads of the
Parcæ, Clotho, Lachesis, and Atropos :

$$a\ddot{\imath}\text{-}\tau\epsilon\ \beta\rho o\tau o\acute{\imath}\sigma\iota$$
$$\gamma\epsilon\iota\nu o\mu\acute{\epsilon}\nu o\iota\sigma\iota\ \delta\iota\delta o\hat{\upsilon}\sigma\iota\nu\ \ddot{\epsilon}\chi\epsilon\iota\nu\ \dot{a}\gamma a\theta\acute{o}\nu\ \tau\epsilon\ \kappa\acute{a}\kappa o\nu\ \tau\epsilon$$
$$a\ddot{\imath}\text{-}\tau\epsilon\ \dot{a}\nu\delta\rho\hat{\omega}\nu\ \tau\epsilon\ \theta\epsilon\hat{\omega}\nu\ \tau\epsilon\ \pi a\rho a\iota\beta a\sigma\acute{\imath}a\varsigma\ \dot{\epsilon}\phi\acute{\epsilon}\pi o\upsilon\sigma\iota$$
$$o\dot{\upsilon}\delta\acute{\epsilon}\pi o\tau\epsilon\ \lambda\acute{\eta}\gamma o\upsilon\sigma\iota\ \theta\epsilon a\grave{\iota}\ \delta\epsilon\iota\nu o\hat{\imath}o\ \chi o\lambda o\hat{\imath}o.$$

(Theog. 218.)

Who to all mortals bring,
With even hand, their lot of good and ill,
Divine pursuers, who are never turned
From their relentless wrath, but keep it still :
Be those they follow men or be they gods.

Later he reads of Hecate, and sees that she is
the real goddess of Destiny, and that the Parcæ
are her servants. At that time few English
scholars would have understood that they repre-

sented the attributes of Destiny : Clotho, her predestinating will ; Lachesis, her distributive power . (Λάχεσις, from λάκη, " a lot ") ; and Atropos, her inflexibility. But he reads :

μοῖραν ἔχειν γαίης τε καὶ ἀτρυγέτοιο θαλάσσης.
* * * *

ἐσθλὴ δ᾽ αὖθ᾽ ὁπότ᾽ ἄνδρες ἀγῶνι ἀεθλεύωσιν,
ἔνθα θεὰ καὶ τοῖς παραγίνεται ἠδ᾽ ὀνίνησι ·
* * * *

καὶ τοῖς, οἱ γλαυκὴν δυσπέμφελον ἐργάζονται
εὔχονται δ᾽ Ἑκατῇ.   (Theog. 413

(That she)
Should for her portion have both earth and sea.
* * * * * *
Supreme wherever men in conflict join,
The goddess loves to risk the issue of
The strife . . . .
Thus to the shrine of Hecate repair
Those who amid the dangers of the deep
Their business find.

So he puts Hecate on the stage, and converts the one witch suggested by Cassandra, into the three suggested by the Parcæ. And in so doing, he not only essays to represent, *in propriâ personâ*, what can only be represented by intermediate agency, for destiny must be shown, as Æschylus shows it, in the life of him who is under its influence. He confounds prophecy with temptation, and invests his witches with the function of the legendary Satan.

Meanwhile, he borrows all his important incidents from the Greek tragedy. Duncan's visit to Macbeth's house is Agamemnon's return home, and Lady Macbeth's pretended loyalty, the ostentatious affection of Clytæmnestra. Then the apparition raised by the witches of the bloody child, and the armed head, and Lady Macbeth's sleep-walking scene, reproduce Cassandra's vision of the children of Thyestes, the coming of Orestes, the avenger, and the murder of Agamemnon. Banquo's ghost, making itself so troublesome in the palace of Macbeth, is evidently suggested by the remark of the chorus, that a ghost will seem to be given of the house of Menelaus; while Clytæmnestra assuring the chorus that she glories in the blood which stains her, finds its parallel in Lady Macbeth showing her bloody hands, and telling her husband that though they are of his colour, yet would she shame to wear a heart so white as his.

We may note, however, before we leave the

play, that the author has taken his incantation scene from Horace's fifth epode, where we have a description of Canidia, the Thracian hag, preparing her philtre :

> Jubet sepulcris caprificos erutas,
>   Jubet cupressus funebres,
> Et uncta turpis ovæa ranæ sanguine,
>   Plumamque nocturnæ strigis,
> Herbasque quas Iolcos atque Iberia
>   Mittit venenorum ferax,
> Et ossa ab ore rupta jejunæ canis
>   Flammis aduri Colchicis.

This he has turned into

> Round about the cauldron go :
> In the poisoned entrails throw, &c.

'Hamlet,' as we have said, is an adaptation of the 'Electra' of Sophocles, which deals with the same fable as 'Agamemnon,' taking that part which describes the vengeance of Orestes. Sophocles employs six characters, besides the chorus, the principal parts being taken by Electra and Chrysothemis, the daughters of Agamemnon and their mother Clytæmnestra. Electra is brave, unselfish, and devoted to the memory of her father; Chrysothemis amiable,

but time-serving. Thus, Electra, though perse-
cuted by Clytæmnestra and her paramour,* on
account of her constant mourning for her father,
scorns to purchase relief by acquiescing in their
crime; while Chrysothemis, anxious to make
the best of things as they are, pays court to
them both. The other characters are Orestes,
Ægisthos, and the Pædagogue of Orestes. The
chorus is composed of Argive maidens. And
those characters, with the Oracle and Pylades,
furnish all the important persons, except
Polonius, in 'Hamlet.' Ægisthos and Clytæmnestra are the King and Queen, Electra and
. Orestes combined make up the character of
Hamlet; while the amiability of Chrysothemis
is personified in Ophelia, and her time-serving in
Rosencrantz and Guildenstern; Pylades supplies
us with the wholly superfluous Horatio, and the
Oracle with the Ghost.†

---

* This description of her condition shows that Cinderella was no
modern idea :

$$\text{ἀλλ' ἄπεα εἴτις ἔποικος ἀναξία,}$$
$$\text{οἰκονομῶ θαλάμους πατρὸς ᾧδε μὲν}$$
$$\text{ἀεικεῖ σὺν στολᾷ}$$
$$\text{κεναῖς δ' ἐφίσταμαι τραπέζαις. (191–4.)}$$

† Though Pylades is not entered among the δράματος προσῶπα,
it is evident he appeared on the stage along with the Pædagogue

And the incidents of the Greek drama suggest the chief incidents in 'Hamlet.' Certain modifications were, of course, necessary in adapting a pagan drama—as will be seen by a brief description of the ' Electra.'

The opening dialogue between the Pædagogue and Orestes describes what had formerly taken place, and refers to the command of the Oracle to avenge the murder of Agamemnon (lines 1 to 85). As it concludes, Electra takes the stage, bewailing the fate of her sire, and denouncing his murderers (86 to 329). To her enters Chrysothemis, who has been sent, like Rosencrantz and Guildenstern, "to pluck out the heart of her mystery" and learn whereto all this lamentation tends. But Electra penetrates her design and throws it in her teeth. One incident of this meeting has, however, been very happily utilised by the English adapter. Chrysothemis has come, bearing in her hands gifts to be laid on the tomb of Agamemnon (330 to 473). And so Ophelia meets Hamlet, carrying the

---

and Orestes at the commencement of the piece, as the former specially addresses him as well as Orestes:

νῦν οὖν, 'Ορέστα καὶ σὺ φίλτατε ξενῶν,
Πυλάδη, τὶ χρὴ δρᾶν ἐν τάχει βουλευτέον. (15, 16.)

presents he had made her, in the happy hours of
love, which she proposes to return, now that
love is dead.

> Their perfume lost . . . .
> Take them again ; for, to the noble mind,
> Rich gifts wax poor, when givers prove unkind.
> <div align="right">(<i>Ilam</i>. III. 1.)</div>

After the departure of Chrysothemis, Clytæmnestra makes her appearance, and much the
same scene ensues as that between Hamlet
and his mother.* And here again the adapter
makes a felicitous use of an incident before
him. As Clytæmnestra says she has had
an ominous dream of Agamemnon's return,
so Hamlet has a second vision of his father's
ghost.

But now the Pædagogue enters (662). He
introduces himself as a messenger, sent by the
King of Phocis, to announce the death of
Orestes, in a chariot-race at the Delphic games.
And that incident seems to have suggested

---

* And his mother uses the very words of Clytæmnestra—

> ὦ, θρέμμ' ἀναιδὲς, σ' ἐγὼ καὶ τἄμ' ἔπη
> καὶ τἄργα τἀμὰ, πολλ' ἄγαν λέγειν ποιεῖ? (624-5.)

> What have I done that thou dar'st wag thy tongue
> In noise so rude against me?

the fencing-match as the means of Hamlet's death and vengeance too. A second scene takes place between the sisters. Chrysothemis arrives (877) in breathless haste to say that Orestes has returned; and, as we read, we seem almost to hear her joyous cry :

Πάρεστ' 'Ορέστης ἡμίν.

She has found offerings on her father's tomb, which must, she thinks, have been placed there by him. But Electra scatters the fond illusion by repeating the announcement that has just been made. She then goes on to propose that, as Orestes is dead, they two should become their father's avengers. But Chrysothemis shrinks from the hazard of such an undertaking, and her reasoning gives the cue for Hamlet's soliloquy on suicide. She would rather " bear the ills they have, than fly to others that they know not of." * She even tries to persuade Electra that they might be very happy if she would only consent to the inevitable. She thus becomes

---

* Ὅρα, κακῶς πράσσοντε, μὴ μείζω κακὰ
κτησώμεθ' . . . .
Οὐ γὰρ θανεῖν ἔχθιστον, ἀλλ' ὅταν θανεῖν
Χρῄζων τὶς, εἶτα μηδὲ τουτ' ἔχῃ λαβεῖν. (Elect. 1009.)

the Ophelia of the Shakespearian tragedy ; while Electra is converted into her contumacious lover. She, indeed, does not tell her sister to go to a nunnery ; but she assures her she must not hope to be married, as Ægisthos will suffer none of their race to increase.

But Chrysothemis gives place to Orestes, who has assumed the character of another envoy from Phocis. He is carrying an urn, which contains, as he tells Electra, the ashes of her brother. Touched, however, by her grief, he makes himself known and avows the purpose for which he has come.

The catastrophe follows soon after, and the drama is at an end.

Now, everybody must see that the adapter has made very felicitous use of the materials afforded by the Greek tragedy ; but no one at all familiar with dramatic literature can fail to perceive at the same time that he was a novice in the art of dramatic composition ; while every classical scholar will be struck by the fact that, though we have much beautiful diction of his own, he nowhere reproduces the splendid declamation of his model. This is evident when we set the two side by side. Take, for

example, the first soliloquy of Hamlet and that
of Electra.

> Oh that this too, too solid flesh would melt,
> Thaw, and resolve itself into a dew ;
> Or, that the Everlasting had not fixed
> His canon 'gainst self-slaughter ! O God ! O God !
> How weary, stale, flat, and unprofitable
> Seem to me all the uses of this world !
> Fye on't, oh ! fye ! 'Tis an unweeded garden
> That grows to seed. Things rank and gross in nature
> Do possess it merely, &c. (I. 2.)

Here the opening is simply ridiculous, suggesting that there is no other alternative to
suicide, but running to water like rotten ice ;
while what follows is tame in comparison with
the sublime strain in which the Greek maiden
utters her grief :

> Ὦ φάος ἁγνὸν καὶ γῆς
> ἰσόμοιρος ἀήρ, ὥς μοι
> πολλὰς μὲν θρήνων ᾠδὰς,
> πολλὰς δ' ἀντήρεις ἦσθον
> στέρνων πλαγὰς αἱμασσομένων
> ὁπόταν δνοφερὰ νὺξ ὑπολειφθῇ ·
> τὰ δὲ παννυχίδων ἤδη στυγεραὶ
> ξυνίσασ' εὐναὶ μογερῶν οἴκων,
> ὅσα τὸν δύστηνον ἐμὸν θρηνῶ
> πατέρα, κ.τ.λ.   (Elect. 86, &c.)

O sacred light, O air, wide as the world,
Thou, thou hast seen the beating of my breasts,
Thou, thou hast heard my cries of woe when night,
The dark-brow'd night, drew back the curtain
That had hid them.   The tears, the groans, .
The unpress'd bed of my detested home,
Bear witness how I mourn my evil-fortuned
Father, &c.

But Hamlet himself suggests that the play was taken, not immediately from the 'Electra,' but from some Italian translation—and such a translation, published in 1588 is still to be found in Dyce's Shakespearian library. Thus, while explaining the play which is going on before the Court, he says, " The story is extant, and written in very choice Italian."   It might, therefore, well be that, in the retranslation of a translation, the rhetorical beauties of the original would be lost.

The next play which has an obviously Grecian original is 'A Midsummer Night's Dream,' the idea of which is borrowed from the story in the Odyssey, which records the adventures of Ulysses in the island of the Cyclops.   Thus Oberon, anointing the eyes of Titania, and depriving her of true vision, is Ulysses putting out the eye of Polyphemus ; while the tricks of

G

the fairies are the tricks of the Satyrs, as we
have them in the 'Cyclops' of Euripides. But
the same fable has furnished the type of all the
fictions which have represented mortals as
falling into the power of supernatural beings.
And 'A Midsummer Night's Dream' is so evidently copied from an Italian drama, that we
shall consider it further under the head of
Italian originals.

Then we have 'Troilus and Cressida,' taken
from the 'Iliad,' and 'Julius Cæsar,' 'Antony and
Cleopatra,' 'Coriolanus' and 'Timon of Athens,'
which are merely dramatizations of Plutarch's
Lives. The famous dialogue between Brutus and
Cassius is, however, a spirited imitation of that
between Agamemnon and Menelaus in the
'Iphigenia in Aulide' of Euripides.

'King Henry IV.' is also largely indebted to
Plutarch, who, in his description of Alcibiades,
supplies the character of Hotspur. Both have
the same boundless ambition, the same recklessness of consequences, the same personal vanity ;
while they are the same in appearance and
influence. Both are the handsomest men of
their time, and both are regarded as models by
their younger companions, who copy even their

defects; for while Alcibiades lisps, Hotspur speaks thick. So Lady Percy avers that her Harry

> Was indeed the glass
> Wherein the noble youths did dress themselves,
> * * * * * *
> And speaking thick, which nature made his blemish,
> Became the accents of the valiant. (2 *Hen. IV.*, II. 3.)

But the likeness goes even further. As Alcibiades disdained to learn to play the flute, because it was an unmanly accomplishment, so Percy

> Would rather be a kitten and cry—mew
> Than one of these same metre-ballad-mongers.
> (1 *Hen. IV.*, III. 1.)

CHAPTER VI.

SPANISH ORIGINALS.

I. The Moorish drama and *Othello*.

II. Drama of the Expulsion and *Merchant of Venice*.

III. Drama of Lopez de Vega and *Romeo and Juliet* and *Much Ado about Nothing*.

DR. JOHNSON, as we have already noted in Chapter I., remarks that the scholars of the Elizabethan age, who studied elegance, read with great diligence the Spanish and Italian poets. And we know that while Petrarch had made English sonneteers, Dante had been the model on which were formed the 'Mirror for Magistrates' and 'The Faïrie Queene.' It is, therefore, only natural to expect that those who devoted themselves to the drama should have sought their models in Spain, where the drama was, and had been for a long time, in a flourishing condition.

But when Shakespeare first appeared the Spanish drama had undergone important vicissitudes; and at least three schools would have presented themselves to the student:

I. The Moorish drama.

II. The drama of the Expulsion period.

III. The drama of Lopez de Vega, who was the contemporary of Shakespeare.

That diversity had, of course, resulted from the political changes which took place between the destruction of the Empire of the West by the barbarians and the accession of Philip II. of Spain in 1556, changes which have been fully discussed by several Spanish and by, at least, one English historian. *

I. After the destruction of the Empire of the West, the Goths established themselves in its several provinces, and having embraced Christianity, became the supporters of the ecclesiastical power, under whose auspices that period of intellectual darkness was inaugurated, which we call the Middle Ages. Towards the close of the

* Robertson's History of Charles V.; Juan Louis Vive's *De Concordia et Discordia in Romano Genere*, Antwerp, 1529; Zurita's *Annales de Aragon ;* Alonso de Ulloa's *Vida del Emperador Carlos V.*, 1568; Adolfo de Castro's *Spanish Protestants*, London, 1851, 12mo.

seventh century, however, the great Saracen
invasion took place, when the south of Spain
was seized by Abdulrahma of Mauritania, one
of the confederate Saracen princes, whose fol-
lowers were thenceforth known as the Moors.
These Moors excelled all their contemporaries in
arts and arms ; and, under their rule, learning
and civilization flourished in Spain, while the
rest of Europe was sunk in ignorance and
barbarism. It was in these days that the
Spanish drama arose and attained its highest
degree of excellence. The principal dramatists
at that time were Jews, invited from Alexandria
by the Moorish rulers, and who became, in fact,
the fathers of Spanish literature.

Some authors, by way of accounting for the
fact of Spanish drama owing so much to the
Roman stage, have asserted that the Spaniards,
meaning of course the Goths settled in Spain,
had addicted themselves to Latin literature
before the advent of the Moors. But, while no
evidence exists to support that hypothesis, such
a fact, if it were a fact, would be opposed to all
we know of the Goths, who, so far from being a
studious people, held learning in contempt, and
omitted no opportunity of destroying its monu-

ments. Alexandrian Scholars, on the other
hand—and the Jews in Spain belonged to that
class—had applied themselves as sedulously to
Latin as to Greek literature, and when called on
to provide plays for Spain, had all that remained
of them from which to choose their models. *
Having to supply entertainment for a grave
people they naturally chose comedy; and the
only comedy available was Roman, the plays of
Aristophanes, the only Greek comedian extant,
being, with one exception ('Plutus'), merely
political skits, which had lost their interest by

---

* At the close of the seventh century, the ancient literature
which remained was such as we now possess, for the Library of
Alexandria, in which all the treasures of Greek and Latin literature
had been stored, was no more. It had been founded by Ptolemæus.
Lagus about 320 B.C., and was afterwards greatly enlarged by his
son, Ptol. Philadelphus. It consisted finally of 700,000 volumes,
400,000 in the library, so called, and 300,000 in the temple of
Jupiter Serapis. A great part of the books in the Library were
burnt during the siege of Alexandria by Julius Cæsar, but were
afterwards replaced by the Library of Pergamus, presented to Cleopatra by Marc Antony. The library in the Serapion remained
until the reign of Theodosius the Great (A.D. 379–395), when it
was destroyed by a fanatic mob of Christians, headed by the archbishop of Alexandria, under pretence of stamping out paganism.
The story of its having been burnt by order of the Caliph Omar,
A.D. 642, is a fable concocted by Abulpharagius. Orosius, the
historian and a Christian priest, *saw the empty shelves* at the close
of the fourth century (see *Mœsta Mundi*, Lugd., 1788; 4to).
Orosius lived from about 455 to 516 A.D.

the effluxion of time. At any rate Plautus and Terence, but especially the former, furnished the dramatic form of the Spanish theatre, which, reaching its zenith in the eighth century, continued to flourish for nearly two hundred years.

The single Elizabethan play translated from the drama of that first great period, is, we believe, the tragedy of 'Othello.' We judge that it is so, partly from its excellence and partly from internal evidence, which points to that date. And no judicious person, we venture to assert, can doubt that it is a histrionic masterpiece, perfect in construction, perfect in character, perfect in dialogue. Then, to our mind, the internal evidence that the original play was Spanish and not Italian, is complete. Of all the world the Venetians exhibited the most violent hatred of the whole Saracen race. Rather than submit to their sway, they had deserted the fertile regions of Italy, and had taken refuge on those barren sand-banks, which ultimately became Venice. To suppose, therefore, that a Moor might be the chosen leader of a Venetian army was to suppose an impossibility. But the minutest details of the play show that its scene was not originally laid in Venice. In Venice the canals are and were always the highways, by which people passed from one place to another; while the universal vehicle of transport was the gondola. Then the private houses faced the water as they do now, having, as a rule, no windows looking upon the streets, which could never have been more than narrow alleys. In 'Othello,' however, the actors pass from place to place along the streets; and, though we are introduced to the Doge and the Council of Ten, and hear of galleys and the Sagittary, neither canals nor gondolas are once mentioned.

But transfer the scene to any town in the south of Spain, between the seventh and eleventh centuries, and everything becomes natural and consistent. There a Moor would be of the ruling class; and an army would necessarily be commanded by one. But the date of the original play might be even later than that we have indicated. The Moorish had been the great days of Spain; and the people looked back to them with affection and pride, long after the dynasty of Abdulrahma had ceased to exist. The dramatist, therefore, who sought to enlist the popular sympathy, would naturally lay his scene in those grand old times.*

Then an early Spanish original of 'Othello' may be inferred from another consideration. Calderon has several plays which bear a striking resemblance to it; but as he did not begin to write till 1622 ('Life of Calderon'), while 'Othello' was performed at the Court Revels in 1604, its author could not have copied Calderon; and it would be absurd to suppose that Calderon copied him. Both, therefore, we think, must have found their original among the early Spanish dramas.

But 'Othello,' in our opinion, was a translation rather than an imitation—that is, until the slaughtering begins. The original, we fancy, was a tragi-comedy, and ended in the discovery of Iago's baseness and the rescue of Desdemona from Othello's suspicion.

As the reader will have gathered from our

---

* So late as the beginning of the sixteenth century, when the Elizabethan stage was almost in view, Alvaro of Cordova complains that the Spanish people so much preferred the Arabic to the Roman literature, that it was " difficult to find, among a thousand persons, one who could write a Latin letter."

remarks, we have been unable to put our hand
on the Spanish piece whose existence we suggest.
We have not even got notice of it from books.
But that need not create any surprise. No
pains were spared to stamp out all traces of the
Moorish dominion ; and its literature must have
been particularly obnoxious to its new Christian
rulers. Thus, though a few copies may have ·
escaped in the hands of individuals, the bulk
was destroyed. Of the few saved, some might
easily have found their way into England,
during the reigns of Mary and Elizabeth, when
both Spanish courtiers and Spanish merchants
were constantly resorting to this country.

II. The second dramatic period dates from the
expulsion of the Moors by Ferdinand and
Isabella to the time of Lopez de Vega. During
that time every means were used by the
authorities to reconcile Spaniards to their
suicidal policy. And the ' Merchant of Venice ' is
obviously founded on some piece written under
that idea. Its object, from first to last, is to
show that a Jew was unworthy of citizenship,
and that neither his wealth nor his family was
entitled to legal protection. And what is the
evidence of Adolfo de Castro, a devout Christian,

of the treatment of the Jews under the Catholic Sovereigns (Ferdinand and Isabella).

"They forged," he says, "the first chains which oppressed the genius of our country. They reduced to ashes more than twenty thousand persons, suspected of maintaining the Jewish religion, and appropriated to themselves the riches of which the accused were plundered by the Inquisition, which gave, to the iniquity of theft the judicial name of confiscation. It was a common saying in Europe that both of these monarchs were actuated by covetousness in persecuting the poor Hebrews, whose complaints against such robberies had reached the Vatican —robberies begun indeed with a show of formal proceedings, but ending in the increase of the royal patrimony, then weakened by the expenses of protracted wars." And in a note he refers to the letter of Sixtus IV. contained in Cantolla's *Compilacion de Buletos de Lumbreras*, addressed by the Supreme Pontiff to Isabella I., in which His Holiness says "Although some persons have whispered something of the kind (royal covetousness) to cover the iniquities of the delinquents, we cannot believe in any injustice on the part of yourself or your illustrious consort." (p. 195.) "In short," he adds, "they expelled from Spain four hundred thousand Jews, a political crime which the blind admirers of Ferdinand and Isabella qualify with the appellation of an heroic resolution to maintain the only true religion in the kingdoms." (p. 196.)

He then proceeds to speak of the destruction of the Arabic literature :

" But the Franciscan Cardinal (Francisco Ximenes de Cisneros), not satisfied with preaching the faith of Christ in this manner (with fire and sword) turned his indignation against the Arabic books found in Granada. Five thousand manuscripts, of which three thousand treated of philosophy and medicine, were burnt to ashes by order of Cisneros; nor would he permit to be first taken off the covers, clasps and ornaments of gold and of pearls, with which they had been bound, although they were demanded and the price of them was offered, viz., ten thousand ducats " (pp. 198, 199).

Again, he says, in the picture of the sixteenth century, which serves as an introduction to his work :

"The Inquisition destroyed all the books which contained doctrines adverse to the opinions and convenience of its judges. Even some works which only threw a glimmering light upon, but did not censure, that pitiable oppression to which Spaniards were reduced, were thrown into the fire ; their titles were put into the indexes, with a view of rendering odious the reading of the few copies which might happen to be miraculously saved from the fury of the Holy Office." (p. li).

And in his appendix he sets out the expurgatorial Index of Cardinal Don Gaspar de Quiroya, archbishop of Toledo and inquisitor-general of Spain (Madrid, 1583), in which no less than seventeen plays are named, besides a

general inhibition of *comedias, tragedias, farsas
ó autos donde se reprende y dize mal de las
personas que frecuentan los sacramentos ó templos,
ó se haze injuria á alguna ordon ó estado aprovado
por la yglesia;* that is, of "comedies, tragedies,
farces or acts, which represents and says evil of
persons who frequent the sacraments or churches,
or are injurious to any order or society approved
by the church" (pp. 375 to 386).

But De Castro could have given us no better
proof, that the Spanish people did not approve
of the bigotry and intolerance of their rulers,
than he has done in setting out a few of the
popular proverbs, which were bandied about
from mouth to mouth in the beginning of the
sixteenth century. One will be sufficient for
our purpose :

> *Roma, Roma la que à los locos doma,
> Y à los cuerdos no perdono.*
>
> Rome tames her fools, 'tis true, but then
> She ne'er forgives her learned men. (p. xxxvii.)

A more literal translation of this will even
still better illustrate our subject :

Rome, Rome, which tames the fools and does not pardon
the wise.

All this shows plainly enough that, if the 'Merchant of Venice' is of Spanish origin, it was founded on ohe of the dramas of the Expulsion period. We will, therefore, proceed to examine the evidence which gives it such an origin. This evidence is external only, but, as we think, conclusive. Thus, Portia is represented as having first seen Bassanio when he visited her father in company with the Marquis of *Montserrat* (I. 2). So also we find among her suitors, the princes of *Morocco* (II. 7) and *Arragon* (II. 9) ; while Antonio trades to *Mexico* (I. 3) a common practice with Spanish, but certainly not of Venetian merchants. Then there is nothing Venetian in the manners and customs introduced, though they agree well enough with Spain. Even at Jessica's elopement, Venetian habits are entirely ignored. No lover serenades her from the water ; no gondola shoots silently into the darkness. Instead of of that, Lorenzo and his party come marching through the streets, disguised as masquers with drum and wry-necked fife ! while Jessica, descending from her window, in the habit of a page, carries a torch before the procession.

But here we are reminded that many have

suggested that Marlowe's 'Jew of Malta' gave Shakespeare the idea of the 'Merchant of Venice ;' and there is, it must be confessed, a striking resemblance between them. In both cases there is a Jew, who has grown rich by usury, who hates Christians and wishes to injure them ; and the Jew's daughter, who loves a Christian and eventually becomes one herself. But there the similarity ends. While Shakespeare has the inconsistencies we have pointed out, Marlowe preserves, in his scene, the manners and customs of Malta as they existed at the time when his drama is supposed to take place, that is, some time after 1530, when Charles V. gave the island to the Knights of St. John. But there is internal evidence that Marlowe had a Spanish original before him. Thus, though Spanish had never been the language in any town of Malta, Barnabas * (the Jew) treats us to more than one specimen of it ; as,

* At the time when Marlowe wrote—say from 1580 to 1592—the country people spoke a kind of corrupt Arabic; while the people of the towns spoke Italian. And that custom prevailed till the beginning of this (nineteenth) century. And the language spoken, at that time, was evidently the result of the political changes which had passed over the island. The first inhabitants, so far as our records go, were Phœnicians; they were driven out by the Greeks, who, in their turn, were ousted by the Carthaginians. The

Bueno para todos mi ganado no era. My gain was not good for all ; (Act II.) and
Hermoso, placer de los dineros. A fine thing to please by money. (Act II.)

For anything we know to the contrary, Shakespeare and Marlowe may have copied the same play, though, as there were doubtless many similar pieces, written between 1492 and 1592, it is by no means necessary to assume as much. Both are libels on the Jewish character and seek to justify an act which is now generally condemned. On that point De Castro's words defy contradiction.

"In Roma herself," he says, "and in the other Italian states, nay, in almost all the polished nations of Europe where Jews live and have lived as they did in Spain, do they not benefit the state by payment of its taxes. And has the residence of Jews endangered the Christian religion ? The prosperity of foreign nations, in which that people are permitted to dwell, demonstrates better than the most powerful arguments, the folly of Catholic sovereigns in expelling them from Spain ; for it cannot be

---

island was then successively taken by the Romans, the Goths, and the *Saracens.* In 1090 it was taken by the Normans ; after them it became an appendage to *Sicily* until 1530, when Charles V. granted it to the knights of St. John, who had been driven by the Turks out of Rhodes. (*Centwell's Gazetteer,* London, 1798, 3 vols. 8vo.)

H

doubted that such expulsion greatly operated against the
nation's prosperity " (p. 196).

III. The third dramatic period lasts from
Lopez de Vega to Calderon ; and from that we
have our ' Romeo and Juliet.' Of this we need
say but little, as its original is identified as one
of De Vega's comedies, translated into English
about the middle of the last century—such
translation being entitled " ' Romeo and Juliet,'
a comedy, written in Spanish by Lopez de
Vega," London, 1770. In this comedy Juliet
wakes when Romeo enters the tomb, and all ends
happily. And it is remarkable that our tragedy,
according to Downes, the prompter, was converted into a comedy, when the play-houses
were reopened after the Restoration. Thus he
tells us that

It was made, some time after 1662, into a tragi-comedy
by Mr. James Howard, he preserving Romeo and Juliet
alive ; so that when it was revived 'twas played alternately
tragical one day and tragi-comical another, for several days
together. (*Johnson's Preface, Steevens' Note*, p. xxxiv.)

CHAPTER VII.

ITALIAN ORIGINALS.

'Midsummer Night's Dream ; ' 'Twelfth Night.'

IT is remarkable that Dr. Johnson had no suspicion that some of Shakespeare's plays were adaptations of Italian dramas. He knew, and has recorded the fact, that such of the Elizabethan scholars, as " united elegance with learning, studied the Spanish and Italian poets with great diligence ; " but there he stops short, influenced, probably, by the consideration that William Shakespeare was not a scholar. He, however, seems to have been very near stumbling on the fact, while remarking on Shakespeare's disregard of the distinctions of different times and place. " He gives," he says, " to one age or nation the customs, institutions and opinions of another. We need not wonder to find Hector quoting Aristotle ('Troilus and Cressida'), when we see the loves of Theseus and Hippolyta com-

bined with the Gothic mythology of fairies ('Midsummer Night's Dream ')." (Preface, p. xxxix.)
Now leaving Aristotle out of the question, the
peculiarity he notices in 'A Midsummer Night's
Dream,' is the peculiarity of most of the early
Italian dramas. And it is quite natural it should
be so. The Goths having become masters of
Italy towards the close of the sixth century,
would, like true barbarians, have insisted on
those they spared adopting their rude super-
stitions, in which fairies occupied a conspicuous
place. When, therefore, their slaves—and all the
Romans spared had been absorbed either in
marriage or servitude—began to compose plays
for their entertainment, they naturally combined
the Roman dramas of their recollection with the
fairy legends they had been compelled to accept,
and as the former were all imitated from the
Greek, that combination arose which is seen in
'A Midsummer Night's Dream.'

And here we must admit that we have been
unable to find any Italian comedy, which can be
given as the original of 'A Midsummer Night's
Dream.' Hence we are inclined to think, it was
an imitation of one of the Italian extemporal
plays exhibited in England in 1578, and to

which we referred in our second chapter. If our thought be correct, Tarleton may have been the Bottom of the first English adaptation, and his extemporal wit is the occasion of Gabriel Harvey's applause. In its original state, we are inclined to believe that the summoning of the Athenian artisans and the tricks of the fairies, constituted the whole of the piece, and that no more was presented to its English audience while it remained an extemporal play.

But if the origin of 'A Midsummer Night's Dream' rests on conjectural grounds, we can identify 'Twelfth Night' with an Italian comedy, entitled *Gli Ingannatori* (The Cheats), printed in 1585. And not only we do so— Shakespeare's contemporaries did the same. Thus we read in the Diary of John Manningham of the Middle Temple as follows :

2 Feb. 1601. At our feast we had a play called Twelve Night, or, What You Will, much like the Comedy of Errors or the Menochmi of Plautus, but most like and near to that in Italian called Inganni.

CHAPTER VIII.

ENGLISH ORIGINALS.

'Henry IV.;' 'Henry VI.;' 'Henry VIII.;' 'Richard III.;' 'King John;' 'King Lear.'

No doubt an abundance of historical information existed when the Shakespearian drama appeared. It was not, however, very trustworthy and did not commend itself to scholars, even at that period.   Most of the chroniclers were monks, who coloured events according as they affected the church, and characters according as they were hostile or subservient to the clergy.   The principal historians were Julius Cæsar the Roman Emperor, the Venerable Bede, Gildas and John Scotus ; Peter of Blois, Ingulph, Endmerus, Turgot, Robert White, William of Malmesbury, Roger de Hovenden, Gervase of Canterbury, Benedict of Peterborough, Henry of Huntingdon, John of Salisbury, and Geoffrey of Monmouth, William Little and Ralph du

Diceto ; Matthew Paris, Thomas Wykes, Walter Hemmingford, Robert d'Avesbury, and Nicholas Trivét ; Walsingham, Otterburne, and Rousse ; Froissart, Philippe de Comines, Argenton and Monstrelet ; Edward Hall, Bale, the biographer of Sir John Oldcastle, Ralph Hollinshed, and John Hooker.

We have set out this long list, in order to show what pains of collation would be required to arrive at a just estimate of characters in the earlier time ; and we may now add, that the Elizabethan dramatists were far from having done so. Thus, the ' Richard III.' of Shakespeare, though it coincided with the opinion of Francis Bacon, did not agree with the opinions of many students of history ; for Sir William Cornwallis, writing in 1600, when the play was in the first flush of its success, observes that :—

Malicious credulity rather embraceth the partial writings of indiscreet chroniclers and witty playmakers, than his (Richard's) laws, and actions, the most innocent and impartial witnesses. (*Ingleby's Centurie of Prayse*, p. 41.)

Then the attempt to blacken the character of Sir John Oldcastle, in the person of Falstaff, elicited so much popular anger, that it was found necessary to disavow such an intention, in the epilogue, where it is said :

> If you be not too much cloyed with fat meat, our humble author will continue the story with Sir John in it, and make you merry with fair Katherine of France ; where for anything I know Falstaffe shall die of a sweat, unless already he be killed with your hard opinions ; for Oldcastle died a martyr ; and this is not the man.
>
> (2 *Henry IV.*)

It cannot, however, be denied that public opinion was justified in supposing that Oldcastle was meant, even if his name were not used at the first representation. He had been the associate of the Prince of Wales, but had fallen into disgrace, on account of his attachment to the opinions of the Lollards, after the Prince became king ; while the real Sir John Falstaff had not. Thus Fuller says of the latter :

> The stage hath been overbold with his memory, making him a Thrasonical puff and emblem of mock valour. True it is that Sir John Oldcastle did first bear the brunt on't, being made the make-sport in all plays, for a coward. It is easily known out of what purse that black penny came, the Papists railing on him for a heretic, and therefore, he must also be a coward. (*Worthies of England—Norfolk*, 1662, C. of P., p. 249.)

The story of 'King Lear' is taken from the Chronicle of Geoffrey of Monmouth, but we are indebted to Shakespeare for the unnecessary horror of Cordelia's murder. A general slaughter of the *dramatis personæ* was, however, his idea of tragedy ; and, if such an important character had been suffered to escape, the piece would probably have been handed down to us as one of Mr. Shakespeare's comedies ; or, at most, as one of his histories. 'Henry VI.' follows Froissart and Hall ; while the others, excepting, perhaps, 'Henry VIII.' which seems to have been written under the influence of popular prejudice, follow the Chronicles of Hollinshed.

CHAPTER IX.

THE ORIGINAL OF SHAKESPEARE'S DRAMATIC FORM AND LANGUAGE.

THAT the dramatic form of the plays was not an inspiration of Shakespeare's own genius, is asserted, in terms, by Shakespeare himself. Thus, when Polonius is introducing the players, whom Rosencrantz had previously identified as Shakespeare's company, by his reference to the Globe (Hercules and his load too) he says "they are the best actors in the world either for tragedy or comedy . . . Seneca cannot be too heavy nor Plautus too light" (Ham. II. 2) a clear intimation that the former was the type of his tragedy, and the latter of his comedy.

Now Seneca's tragedies are barren of action, consisting for the most part of declamation, in which bombast and exaggeration take the place of true sublimity. And that is the character which Dr. Johnson assigns to Shakespeare's tragedy.

"In it," he says, "his performance seems to be constantly worse as his labour is more. The effusions of passion, which exigence forces out, are, for the most part, striking and energetick ; but whenever he solicits his invention or strains his faculties, the offspring of his throes is tumour, meanness, tediousness, and obscurity" (p. xl).

And Warton, in his 'History of English Poetry,' holds the same view, when he rates the pure declamation of Gorboduc above " the false sublime introduced by Shakspeare to please the vulgar." And it does not affect the argument to admit, as all must admit, that any one of Shakepeare's tragedies, if we omit 'Titus Andronicus,' is far more interesting than Lord Buckhurst's more correct work. The correct is not always entertaining ; and we are most of us vulgar enough to prefer entertainment to the rules of propriety.

The blending of comedy with tragedy is not a peculiarity of Seneca; but the mingling of tragedy with comedy is a striking feature of Plautus ; so that to that extent, the Roman comedian becomes the type of the English tragedy, the one being *comico-tragœdia,* as the other was *tragico-comœdia,* a mere inversion that scarcely amounts to a difference.

In one important particular, however, the dramatic form of Shakespeare's tragedy has no warrant in Seneca, nor in any of the Greek tragedians he copied. Neither the one nor the other justifies the wholesale slaughter of the *dramatis personæ* in which Shakespeare indulged.

Greek tragedy, as its history shows, had no necessary connection with slaughter. The word was originally used to describe the rude choruses, sung by the Bacchanals, which though sometimes called ‵διθύραμβοι, or songs of Bacchus (Διθύραμβος), were more frequently designated by τραγῷδιοι, or songs of the goat (τράγος), that animal being the special sacrifice offered to Bacchus and always forming a prominent object in his festivals.* From all we know of those songs, they seem to have been very similar to

---

* We learn from Herodotos (lib. ii.) that the worship of Bacchus was introduced into Greece from Egypt, where he was known as Osiris, by Melampus. This Melampus, if he ever lived at all, must have lived before Lycurgus, King of Thrace, a monarch who, by severe laws, endeavoured to abolish the worship of Bacchus—that is, to put an end to drunkenness—by destroying all the vines in Thrace and forbidding the planting of fresh ones. The origin of tragedy therefore dates from a period antecedent to our chronology; because Lycurgus is referred to in the ‘Iliad’ as having attempted the destruction of the Bacchic culture before the Trojan war. Thus—

> ′Ος ποτε μαινομένοιο Διωνύσσοιο τιθήνας
> Σεῦε, κατ’ ἠγάθεον Νυσσήιον. (*Il.* VI. 132–3.)

“When he drove the nurses of the mad-brained Dionysus (Bacchus) into the sacred retreats of Nyssie.”

our old-fashioned negro minstrelsy, disconnected tirades, full of impudent allusions, and accompanied by the grotesque humour proper to those who were drunk. Nor were the Bacchanals themselves very different in appearance to our earlier sable songsters. They were, indeed, more inclined to strip themselves than to assume a burlesque costume; and they discoloured their faces with wine-lees instead of lamp-black; but they sang and danced to the lyre and tambourine as our friends danced and sang to the tambourine and banjo.

In that state tragedy seems to have remained till the sixty-first Olympiad, or 536 B.C., when Thespis took it in hand. But, though he added something to it, he did not alter its form. Thus Horace tells us that:

He is said to have found us people ignorant of tragic verse; that he carried his poems about in country waggons, those who sang and acted having their faces daubed with wine-lees.

> Ignotum tragicæ genus invenisse Camenæ
> Dicitur, et plaustris vexisse poëmata Thespis,
> Qui canerent agerentque peruncti fæcibus ora.
>
> (*Ars Poët.* 275, &c.)

In other words, he introduced the episode, or a narrative in verse, which he added to the song.

Horace records no further change until the time of Æschylus (B.C. 479) :

After him (Thespis) Æschylus, the inventor of the masque and the becoming tunic, covered the stage with a roof, and taught (the actors) to declaim in a sublime strain and strut in buskins.

> Post hunc, personæ pallæque repertor honestæ
> Æschylus, et modicis instravit pulpita tignis,
> Et docuit magnum loqui nitique cothurno.
> (*Ars Poët.* 278, &c.)

These were very important alterations, especially as the introduction of the masque was the introduction of different characters.

Then, if we examine his tragedies, we find that he converted the episode from a simple poem into a regular drama, and changed the dithyrambic songs of the chorus into odes illustrative of the drama, or comments on it from a popular point of view. Meanwhile the distinguishing characteristic of tragedy was henceforth *its severely correct literary style.* It was, as Horace says, *magnum loqui,* to talk big instead of using the vernacular, which was good enough for comedy. And now, we may be sure, the etymology of the word was taken as altered. And it required no violence to alter it. If

τράγος signified a goat, it also signified the
odour of virility and τραγῳδίαι (tragedy) might,
therefore, as properly represent a work of
matured genius, as the ranting choruses of the
rabble, which had followed the goat with the
gilded horns. And from that time forward it
, was entrusted with the highest function of
civilized life. Its λογείον or stage became
thenceforth a teacher's platform, and its dramas
sermons which dispensed those moral truths so
long concealed under the symbolism of religious
ceremony. But at no time, neither in its rudest
nor in its most polished form, had it any
necessary connection with death. In the former,
it had aimed at the promotion of fun and frolic ;
in the latter, though it might introduce death in
the commission or punishment of crime, its
object was to uphold virtue and discountenance
vice. The indiscriminate slaughter therefore,
which distinguishes Shakespeare's, and which
has become so completely the characteristic of
modern . tragedy, that it has made the word
itself a synonym of violent death, owes its
existence not to the canons of antiquity, but to
an unworthy pandering to the depraved taste of
more modern times.

The origin of the dramatic form of SHAKE-SPEARE'S COMEDY is, however, entirely ancient. It is, in fact, a reproduction of the comedy of Plautus, and of Plautus alone ; and a comparison of the two will put the assertion beyond doubt.

"Shakspeare," as Dr. Johnson says, "is, above all modern writers, the poet that holds up to his hearers a faithful mirror of manners and of life. His characters are not modified by the customs of particular places, unpractised by the rest of the world, nor by the accident of transient fashions and temporary opinions, but are the genuine progeny of common humanity such as the world will always supply."

(p. xxviii.)

And Dunlop says of Plautus, that he was so completely the poet of nature, that, much as manners, and even language, had changed between his time and the time of Diocletian —a period of five hundred years—he was still the favourite of the Roman stage in Diocletian's reign. (*History of Roman Litera-ture*, I. 230.)

Again Dr. Johnson remarks of Shakespeare that :

His scenes are occupied only by men, who act and speak as the reader thinks he should himself have spoken or acted on the same occasion. Even when the agency is supernatural, the dialogue is level with life. He has not only shown human nature as it acts in real exigencies, but as it would be found in trials to which it cannot be exposed (p. xxxi).

And that must also be said by any one who takes up Plautus's comedy of 'Amphitryo.' In it the plot supposes that Jupiter has fallen in love with Alcmena, the wife of Amphitryo, and visits her in the shape of her husband, accompanied by Mercury in the form of Sosia, Amphitryo's slave, and the first scene finds the real Sosia applying for admission at his master's house ; while Mercury, who is acting as doorkeeper, repels him as an impostor. And thus the dialogue runs :—

Sosia. Quis ego sum saltem, si non sum Sosia?—te interrogo.

Mer. Ubi ego Sosia nolim esse, tu esto sanè Sosia.

Nunc quando ego sum, vapulabis ni hinc abis, ignobilis.

Sosia. Certo (edepol), quòm illum 'contemplo et formam cognosco meam

Quemadmodum ego sæpè in speculum inspexi, nimis simili 'st mei.

Itidem habet petasum ac vestitum, tam consimili 'st atque ego

Sura, pes, statura, tonsus, oculi, nasum vel labra,

Malæ, mentum, barba, collum ; totus ! quid verbis opu' st?

I

Si tergum cicatricosum, nihil hoc simile 'st similius ;
Sed quòm cogito equidem certo idem sum qui semper
    fui.
Novi herum ; novi ædeis nostras.   Sane sapio et
    sentio.
Non ego illi obtempero quod loquitur ; pultabo forcis.

Mer.   Quò agis te ?

Sosia.   Domum.

Mer.   Quadrigas si nunc inscendas Jovis
Atque hinc fugias, ita vix poteris effugere infortunium.

Sosia.   Nonne, heræ meæ nuntiare quod herus meus jussit,
    licet ?

Mer.   Tuæ, si quid vis nuntiare : hanc nostram adire non
    sinam.
Nam, si me irretassis, hodie lumbifragium hinc auferes.

Sosia.   Abeo potius.   Dii immortales ! obsecro vostram
    fidem.   (282–299, &c.)

Sos.   Who am I, if I am not Sosia, I pray you ?

Mer.   When I don't wish to be Sosia, you shall be he.
Now when I am, you will be beaten if you don't go
    away, you vagabond.

Sos.   By Pollux, when I look at him I recognise myself
As I have often seen it in the mirror.   He's
    extremely like me.
He has the hat and clothes, and everything just as
    ᴠI have—
Leg, foot, figure, hair, eyes, nose, even lips,
Cheeks, chin, beard, neck—What's the use of talking?
If he has a back well scored with stripes, nothing
    can be more like—
Yet, when I think, I am certainly the same that I
    have always been.

I know my master; I know our home—I can smell
and feel.

I won't give in to what he says. I shall knock at
the door (*knock*).

Mer. Whither are you going?

Sos. Home.

Mer. Now if you were to get
into Jupiter's four-horse chariot,

And were to cut away, you'd scarcely be able to
avoid a misfortune.

Sos. Mayn't I tell my mistress what my master has
commanded?

Mer. You may tell anything you like to *your* mistress;
but I shan't suffer you to bother mine.

And if you irritate me, you'll carry a broken back
away with you.

Sos. I'll much rather go (*retiring*). O immortal gods!
I implore your protection.

Such an incident as this could not happen; but
if it were possible, would not the dialogue be
very similar?

But if Plautus be the model of the dramatic
form of Shakespeare's comedies, he is only a
secondary model; for both Terence and he had
a model in the New Greek comedy. The MSS.
of the former state so much on the face of them.
Thus they say that the *Hecyra* is taken from
Apollodorus, and the *Heautontimoroumenos* and
Eunuchus from Menander; while we read in

the prologue to the *Mercator* of Plautus, that it is the *Emporos* of Philemon.

> Græcè hæc vocatur *Emporos* Philemonis,
> Eadem, Latinò, *Mercator* Marci Accii.   (9, 10.)

And the fragments of Philemon which we possess * show that the humour of Plautus is essentially that of Philemon.   Take No. XII. as an example.

> *Λ.* τίς ἐστιν οὗτος;
> *B.*   ἰατρός.
> *Λ.*   ὡς κακῶς ἔχει
> ἅπας ἰατρὸς, ἄν κακῶς μηδεὶς ἔχῃ.

> *Λ.* Who is this?
> *B.*   A physician.
> *Λ.*   How ill is
> Every physician, if nobody is ill!

Now Seneca, like Plautus and Terence, worked from excellent models; but that happened to him which happens to all inferior workmen.   While they succeeded in reproducing

---

* The fragments we possess are only sufficient to make us regret that we have no more. Menander is said to have written one hundred and eight comedies; yet we have only fragments amounting in all to one hundred and five lines; while of Philemon we have seventy lines, of Apollodorus twenty-two, of Philippides six, of Diphilus eighteen, and of Posidippus nineteen.

the spirit as well as the form of their models, he only reproduced the outline of his.   Hence it is that Shakespeare's comedy is so much superior to his tragedy.

As regards the LANGUAGE OF SHAKESPEARE, it may be thought unnecessary to go behind Shakespeare himself.   And so it would be, if it did not stand out in such strong relief from the language of his contemporaries; but in this respect, also, he is *unus inter omnes*; and it does not happen that one author, superior as he may be in style, is totally unlike his fellows, unless he has adopted a model which they have ignored.   We are, therefore, justified in asking who was his.   And the answer, in our opinion, must be ARISTOTLE, the prince of syllogism—the great master of proverbial philosophy.   We were first led to associate him with Shakespeare from a remark in his rhetoric, concerning the practice of PREDICTION.   He says (Phil. VII. 5) that one of the augurs of his day declared that the *future* being obscure, while the *past* was easy to know, his predictions of the future were based on the occurrences of the past.   The following passage in 2 Henry IV., III. 1, imme-diately occurred to us :—

There is a history in all men's lives
Figuring the nature of the *times deceased*,
The which observed, a man may *prophesy*,
With a near aim, of the main chance of things
As yet not come to light.   (2 *Hen. IV.*, III. 1.)

And a very slight examination of the Ethics convinced us that the ancient Stagyrite was also the type of Shakespeare's language. When, therefore, in looking through a Shakespeariana, we came upon 'Illustrations of Aristotle from the Dramatic Works of Shakespeare,' by J. Esmond Riddle, M.A., Oxford, 1832, we hailed the book as a friend that would save us further research. But the hope has been disappointed. The little post 8vo of 134 pages lies ·open before us; and it does nothing of the sort. There are one hundred and fifty-eight extracts from Aristotle, taken from the 'Ethics' and the 'Rhetoric,' arranged under the heads of Moral Sense, Anger, Indignation, Hatred, Jealousy, Injury, &c., but not one parallel passage from Shakespeare. Thus his first extract from the 'Ethics' is :—

Οἱ μοχθηροὶ—ἑαυτοὺς φεύγουσιν· ἀναμιμνήσκονται γὰρ πολλῶν καὶ δυσχερῶν, καὶ τοιοῦθ' ἕτερα ἐλπίζουσι, καθ' ἑαυτοὺς ὄντες—μεταμελείας οἱ φαυλοῖ γέμουσιν. (*Eth.* IX. 4.)

To illustrate that he quotes from ' Macbeth'
(II. 2), beginning, " This is a sorry sight," down
to " Making the green one, red."   Also III. 2,
beginning, " Let the frame of things," down to
" restless ecstasy."   Also ' Hamlet,' III. 3, beginning, " O my offence is rank," down to " all
may be well."   And ' Othello,' V. 2, beginning,
" Where should Othello go?" down to " O
Desdemona, Desdemona! dead!"

Now that is merely illustrating an *idea*; and
ideas are common property, and may be found
in any author.   Let us, however, translate the
Greek philosopher to see if we can't find similar
expressions in Shakespeare.

The criminal persecute themselves; for they
think of many difficulties and expect the same
things, in another place, on their own account.
Wicked men heap up regrets.

What is this but the type of:—

If it were done, when 'tis done, then 'twere well
*   *   *   *   But in these cases,
We still have judgment here; that we but teach
Bloody instructions, which, being taught, return
To plague the inventor.   This even-handed justice
Commends the ingredients of our poison'd chalice
To our own lips.   (*Macb.* I. 7.)

CHAPTER X.

THE MIND OF SHAKESPEARE.

THE mind of Shakespeare, like that of any other author, must mean his judgment. It should, therefore, reveal itself throughout an author's works. That, however, is not a characteristic of Shakespeare's plays. They display important differences on the most similar points. 'Hamlet' and 'Othello' both treat of love and anger; yet how differently they judge of these passions! In the latter love is described as a thing the author has felt, and we know he judges it to be real as he watches the retreating form of Desdemona.

> Excellent wretch, perdition catch my soul
> But I do love thee! (*Oth.* III. 3.)

But the former describes it rather as a phenomenon he has observed, and keeps his judgment suspended between reality and appearance.

Ham. I did love you once.
Oph. Indeed, my lord, you made me believe so.
Ham. You should not have believed me ; for virtue cannot
      so inoculate our old stock, but we shall relish of
      it. I loved you not.   (*Ham.* III. 1.)

An equal diversity is perceptible in their
delineation of anger. Hamlet is merely rhetorical when he exclaims :

                  Ere this,
  I should have fatted all the region kites
  With this slave's offal. Bloody, bawdy villain !
                    (*Ham.* II. 2.)

And he evidently feels he is no more, for he
immediately adds :

  Why, what an ass am I ! This is most brave
  That I, the son of a dear father murdered,
  Must, like a whore, unpack my heart with words
  And fall a cursing like a very drab. .   (*Ham.* II. 2.)

But we can see Othello is quivering with
passion as he cries :

            If I do prove her haggard,
  Tho' that her jesses were my dear heart-strings,
  I'd whistle her off.   (*Oth.* III. 3.)

No doubt there is an apparent unanimity in
most of the plays ; but so there is in the

literature of every age—an unanimity due, not to identity of judgment, but to the general knowledge then existing, the linguistic fashion of the period and its habitual tone of thought; and that is the unanimity which characterizes the general structure of the plays which, on a close inspection, reveal the divergences we have pointed out, and which, in other cases, discover the presence of different authors. Still there are *passages*, in nearly all the pieces, which the merest novice would recognise as the work of one and the same mind; though, so far from being always characteristic of the pieces in which they occur, they are frequently in strong contrast to them. Those passages, however, constitute all that can properly be called the mind of Shakespeare.

And the first, and perhaps the most striking, quality on which that mind is formed consists in a weak animal development. This is the more remarkable because, at that time, the life even of scholars and poets was distinctly animal. Of course there were temperate and virtuous people among them, like Chapman and Samuel Daniel, but the general life was gross and sensual, and only refined, if refinement be not a misnomer, by sexual passion. Yet Shakespeare, in the selected passages to which we have referred, manifests a total insensibility to the gross passion of love. In descriptions of Platonic affection and conventional gallantry he is unsurpassed ; but when he essays to be personally tender, his muse becomes tediously perfunctory, as we see it in Hamlet. Then his intense abhorrence of intemperance and personal defilement is another proof of super-animal organisation, in which he seems to stand alone. In what other author of the time do we read anything like his intense loathing of them which we find in Julius Cæsar?

> To sit
> And keep the turn of tippling with a slave !
> To reel the streets at noon and stand the buffet
> With knaves that smell of sweat !   (I. 4.)

It may be said that his love of music, of flowers and of perfume, was a wholly sensuous love ; but he associates it with sublime ideas which animal natures never do ; as in the following :

> That strain again ; it had a dying fall.
> Oh ! it came o'er my ear like the sweet South
> That breathes upon a bank of violets,
> Stealing and giving odour.   (*Twelfth Night*, I. 1.)

But if deficient in animal activity, his intellectual faculties seem to have obtained the highest point of development. Hence his judgment differs so widely from that of his contemporaries. They saw the same persons as he did, and lived in the same world; but, while they only comprehended the outer form of men and things, his keener observation discovered the nature which lay hid under the temporary fashions and circumstances of both. This is the real secret of his immortality. As Aubrey, the antiquarian, said so early as the middle of the seventeenth century: "His comedies will remain wit as long as the English tongue is understood, for that he handles *mores hominum*. Now our present writers reflect so much upon particular persons and coxcombries, that twenty years hence they will not be understood."

With this attempted explanation of the mind of Shakespeare we shall conclude our sketch of the characteristics of the plays. We have been thus particular in analysing them, because the surest guide to the personality of a disputed authorship will be found in his works.

CHAPTER XI.

THE AUTHORSHIP OF THE PLAYS.

Their Publication in 4to—Folio of 1623—Shakespeare's
Name no Evidence of Authorship.

In these days the publication of a book generally leads to the discovery of its author; and
it is, at least, remarkable that the publication of
Shakespeare's plays did not decide that important
point. But instead of settling the question, it
seem to have opened it. Our critic's explanation of the anomaly is most unsatisfactory.

"So careless," he says, "was this great poet of future
fame, that, though he had retired to ease and plenty while he
was yet little declined into the vale of years, before he could
be disgusted with fatigue or disabled by infirmity, he made
no collection of his works, nor desired to rescue those that
had been already published, from the depravations that
obscured them, or to secure to the rest a better destiny, by
giving them to the world in their genuine state."

(*Preface*, p. lxi.)

But the answer is, that no great poet ever

was, or, ever could be insensible to future fame.
If, however, Shakespeare were not the author, but
only the purchaser of them, and if he had sold
his interest to the other players, his conduct was
perfectly natural.   And this view is strengthened
by the fact, that he *did* publish as his own, the
poems of ' Venus and Adonis ' and ' The Rape of
Lucrece.'

But the circumstances under which the plays
were published by other people are, in themselves, remarkable.   Twenty pieces were printed
in 4to during his life, of which twelve *bore his
name !* viz. :

Love's Labour Lost	1598
A Midsummer Night's Dream . .	1600
Merchant of Venice	—
Henry IV., 2nd Part . . .	—
Much Ado about Nothing . . .	—
Merry Wives of Windsor . . .	1602
Hamlet	1603
Othello	1604
King Lear	1608
Pericles of Tyre	1609
Troilus and Cressida	—
King John	1611

And eight were published without the name
of any author, viz. :

Henry VI., 2nd Part	.	.	.	1595
Richard II.	.	.	.	.	1597
Richard III.	.	.	.	.	—
Romeo and Juliet (1st ed.)	.	.	—
Henry IV., 1st Part	.	.	.	1598
Romeo and Juliet (2nd ed.)	.	.	1599
Henry VI., 3rd Part	.	.	.	1600
Titus Andronicus	.	.	.	.	—
Henry V.	.	.	.	.	.	—
Romeo and Juliet (3rd ed.)	.	.	1609

In thus selecting some to bear his name and others to be published anonymously, there is, at least, a suggestion that the claim to authorship was not without danger. And though the first copyright act, which vested the sole right of publication for a period of fourteen years, in the author or his assigns, was not passed till 1709 (8 Anne, cap. 19), to publish a book as the work of one man, when it was the work of another, would have constituted a fraud, of which the Court of Chancery would have taken cognizance under the ordinary rules of equity. And the circumstances attending the publication of 'Romeo and Juliet' suggest, if not an application to the Court for an injunction, the threatening of such a proceeding.! Some time after 1609 a fourth 4to edition was published without

any date, but with the name of William Shakespeare as author. But what happened? After
a few copies had been sold, Shakespeare's name
was withdrawn ; and the rest of the impression
was issued anonymously. (' New Shakespeare
Society' Series II. Daniel's ' Romeo and Juliet,'
Parallel Texts of the first two 4to's. London.
1874. Introduction, p. iv.)

Some twelve or thirteen years after that
event, however, when Shakespeare had been dead
seven years, that is, in 1623, the players
published the first folio edition, containing all
the plays they acknowledged as Shakespeare's ;
and in that they included ' Romeo and Juliet.'
The title is as follows :

Mr. William Shakespeare's Comedies, Histories and
Tragedies, published according to the true original copies.
London, printed by Isaac Jaggard and Ed. Blount, 1623.

To the plays so published were prefixed a
Dedication to the Earls of Pembroke and
Montgomery, and an Address to the reader,
both signed by Hemynge and Condell, the
players, and certain laudatory verses composed
by Ben Jonson. The Address is as follows :

To the Great Variety of Readers.

From the most able to him that can but spell there you
are numbered. We had rather you were weighed,
especially when the fate of all books depends upon your
capacities and not of your heads alone but of your purses.

Well, it is now public and you will stand for your
privileges, we know, to read and censure. Do so; but buy
it first. That doth best commend a book, the stationer
saith. Then how odd soever your brains be or your wisdom,
make your license the same and spare not. Judge your
six-pen'orth, your shillingsworth, your five-shillingsworth at a
time or higher, so you rise to the just rates and welcome.
But, whatever you do buy, censure will not drive a trade
nor make the Jacke go. And though you be a magistrate
of wit and sit on the stage of Blackfriars or the Cock-pit to
arraign plays daily, know these plays have had their trial
already and stood out all appeals and do now come forth
quitted rather by a decree of Court than any purchased
letters of commendation. It had been a thing, we confess,
worthy to have been wished that the author himself had lived
to have set forth and overseen his own writings; but since
it hath been ordained otherwise and he by death departed
from that right, we pray you do not envy his friends the
office of their care and pains, to have collected and
published them; and so to have published them, as, where
(before) you were abused with diverse stolen and surreptitious copies, maimed and deformed by the frauds and
stealths of injurious impostors that exposed them, even
those are now offered to your view cured and perfect of
their limbs and all the rest absolute in their numbers, as he
conceived them, who, as he was a happy imitator of nature,
was a most gentle expresser of it. His mind and hand
went together, and what he thought he uttered with that

K

easiness, that we have scarce received from him a blot in
his papers. But it is not our province who only gather his
works and give them you, to praise him; it is yours that
read him. And there we hope, to your diverse capacities,
you will find enough both to draw and hold you; for his
wit can no more be hid than it could be lost. Read him
therefore and again and again; and if then you do not like
him, surely you are in some manifest danger not to understand him. And so we leave you to other of his friends,
whom, (sic) if you need, can be your guides. If you need
them not, you can lead yourselves and others. And such
readers we wish him.   JOHN HEMYNGE,
                                  HENRIE CONDELL.

Now it may be said, that the title of the
book does not claim the authorship for Mr.
Shakespeare, and that they were his in the sense
that he had put them on the stage, or, that he
had purchased them, or, that he had done both.
But the players' Address to the readers distinctly
affirms that he composed them; while Ben
Jonson's verses infer as much. We say " infer,"
because he does not tell us that Shakespeare was
the William Shakespeare of Stratford-on-Avon;
and, as we shall presently see, Shakespeare was a
name sometimes used without reference to
authorship. The Address, however, tells us
more. It affirms that the 4to editions were
" stolen and surreptitious copies, maimed and
deformed by the frauds and stealths of injurious

impostors that exposed them ; " while they
infer that Shakespeare had not sanctioned the
publication. We see, therefore, that although
some of the 4to editions (the twelve that we have
set out) described him as the author, he did not
thereby claim the authorship ; but that, on the .
contrary, he had died and made no sign. Nevertheless, it is evident that in 1623, those who
knew Shakespeare best, represented to the world
that he was the author of the thirty-six dramas
contained in the Folio copy.

But if the players were legally seized of those
plays, as, no doubt they were, they must have
become possessed of them during Shakespeare's
life ; for there is no mention of them in his will.
Why, then, did they wait till seven years after
his death, before they print them ? Were they
waiting until the effluxion of time should
relieve them from the apprehension of such
protests as had been made in the case of the
fourth 4to edition of ' Romeo and Juliet ' ? And
what events had happened between the first appearance of the plays and 1623 ? Certainly not
less than fifteen persons, contemporary authors
or actors had departed this life and were silenced
for ever. Richard Tarlton had died in 1588 ;

Robert Greene, in 1592; Christopher Marlowe, in 1593; James Burbage, in 1597; John Lyly and George Peele, in 1598; Edmund Spenser, in 1599; Thomas Nash, in 1600; Dekkar, in 1609; Barnfield and Francis Beaumont in 1615; Philip Henslowe, in 1616; Richard Burbage and Sir Walter Raleigh, in 1618; and Samuel Daniel in 1619.

The publication of the plays, however, cannot be taken as more conclusive, when made by the players, than when undertaken by anybody else; and the booksellers published, as his, no less than eleven plays which the players repudiated; viz:

1. Arden of Feversham	. . .	1592
2. Locrine	. . . .	1595
3. Edward III.	. . .	1596
4. Sir John Oldcastle	. . .	1600
5. Thomas Ld. Cromwell	. . .	1602
6. The London Prodigal	. . .	1605
7. The Puritan	. . . .	1607
8. The Yorkshire Tragedy	. . .	1608
9. Pericles of Tyre	. . .	1609
10. Noble Kinsmen	. . . .	1634
11. Birth of Merlin	. . . .	1662

But there is positive evidence, if prejudice would allow us to accept it, that the application of Shakespeare's name to certain works is no necessary proof that he wrote them. Thus the first publisher of the 'Sonnets,' though he describes them on the title-page as "Shakespeare's Sonnets," distinctly affirms, in a sort of dedication, that a Mr. W. H. was "the only begetter of them." Shakespearian critics have, of course, pretended that "the only begetter" does not mean author; but the term is used to signify "author" in the case of William Shakespeare himself. Thus, John Weaver, writing two years after the publication of 'Venus and Adonis,' says, in his *Ode ad Gulielmum Shakespeare*, 1595 :

> Honey-tongued Shakspeare when I saw thine *issue*,
>   I swore Apollo *got* them and none other,
> Rose-cheeked Adonis and his amber tresses
>   Fair, fire-hot Venus charming him to love her, &c.
>   (*C. of P.*)

And Ben Jonson uses the same figure, in the verses prefixed to the first Folio, when he says :

>   Look, how the *father's* face
> Lives in his *issue* /   Even so the race
> Of Shakspeare's mind and manners brightly shines,
> In his well turnèd and true-filèd lines.

The publication of the plays did not, therefore, settle the question of authorship.

CHAPTER XII.

AUTHORSHIP OF THE PLAYS, CONTINUED.

The Character to be expected of the Author—Contemporary Opinion of the Genius of Shakespeare.

IF we give due effect to the characteristics of the plays, what is the character we should expect of their author? Is it that of an untutored genius, following a degraded calling? Is it not rather that of a genius, enriched by all the advantages of education? Are we not bound to expect, not only an erudite scholar, but a philosopher, whose opinions soared above the prejudices which still enthralled vulgar minds? But was such the opinion contemporaries entertained of William Shakespeare, the actor? Let us turn for an answer to "The Centurie of Prayse," a work which its author, the late Dr. Ingleby, modestly described as the materials for a history of opinions respecting the popular bard. It contains every allusion he could find in authors living in the century comprised between 1592 and 1692.*

And in what he calls the Forespeech he candidly allows, that Shakespeare's immediate contemporaries expressed no great admiration for either him or his works.

"The absence," he says, "of ,sundry great names, with which no pains of research, scrutiny, or study could connect the most trivial allusion to the bard or his works, such, *e.g.*, as Lord Bacon, Selden, Sir John Beaumont, Henry Vaughan and Lord Clarendon, is *tacitly significant;* and the iteration of the same vapid and affected compliments, couched in conventional terms, from writers of the two first periods (1592–1641) comparing Shakspeare's tongue, vein, or pen to silver, honey, sugar or nectar, while they ignore his greatest distinguishing characteristic, is *expressly significant.* It is plain, for one thing, that the bard of our admiration was unknown to the men of that age; though it is undeniable that his supremacy, in some important respects, was at length recognised by Ben Jonson, and subsequently by Milton and Dryden. Assuredly no one, during the century, had any suspicion that the genius of Shakspeare was unique, and that he was *sui generis, i.e.* the only exemplar of his species. Those, who ranked him very

---

* The author seems at first to have made the century begin in 1589, taking an allusion to *Hamlet*, made in that year, as the beginning of the series. For some reason or other, into which we need not now enter, that allusion was transferred to a list of exclusions at the end of the work, thus leaving an allusion in 1592 at the head of the series.

high, compared him to Spenser, Sidney, Chapman, Jonson, Fletcher, and even lesser lights ; and most of the judges of that time assigned the first place to one of them " (pp. x–xi).

In one unimportant particular the above is inaccurate. Though Bacon never mentions the name of Shakespeare, he does refer to one of his plays. Thus, in his charge against Mr. Oliver St. John we have : " And, for your comparison with Richard II., I see you follow the example of them, that brought him upon the stage in Queen Elizabeth's time." (*Bacon's Works*, iv. 439). Our conclusion, however, must be that the " vapid compliments " referred to the poems he published in 1593 and 1594, and that no one, qualified to judge, regarded him as the author of those of the plays which really deserved much commendation.

But, as we have pointed out, Dr. Ingleby has ignored the first reference made to the Shakespearian drama ; and we cannot help saying that he did so because it contradicts the claim of Shakespeare in plain terms. Lord Campbell, however, thought it of sufficient importance to be a sort of text for his book, entitled ' Shakespeare's Legal Acquirements,' a work undertaken at the suggestion of Mr. James

Payne Collier, who had formed the opinion that Shakespeare, considering the internal evidence of legal knowledge, must have been a lawyer's clerk before he became an actor.

The reference is contained in an "Address to the gentlemen students of the Two Universities," by Thomas Nash, prefixed to Greene's 'Menaphon,' 1589, and is to the following effect :

I will turn back to my first studies of delight and talk a little in friendship with our trivial translators.* It is a common practice now-a-days among a sort of shifting campanions, that run through every art and thrive by none, to learn the trade of *Noverint, in which they were born*, and busy themselves with the endeavours of art, that could scarce latinize their neck-verse, if they had need. Yet English Seneca read by candle-light, yields many good sentences ; as "Blood is a beggar" and so forth ; and if you entreat him fair, on a frosty morning, he will afford you whole *Hamlets*, I should say handfuls of tragical speeches. But, oh! grief! *tempus edax rerum*, and what is that will last always? The sea, exhaled by drops, will in continuance be dry ; and Seneca, let blood line by line and page by page, at length must die to our stage. ('Shakespeare's Legal Acquirements.')

* From this we may infer that gentlemen of both the Universities were in the habit of translating plays, which translations they sold to the actors.

Here we have a sufficiently explicit statement, that the author of 'Hamlet' was a lawyer and the son of a lawyer ; for, as Lord Campbell says—though most of us knew it before—the trade of *Noverint* meant the legal profession, deeds having always begun, in earlier times, with the words *Noverint universi per presentes*, " Know all men by these presents."

Now it must be obvious, that Nash did not refer to William Shakespeare, there being no pretence for saying that his father was a lawyer. Lord Campbell, it is true, overlooks that fact, but contents himself with supposing that the 'Hamlet' referred to was an earlier play than ours.   We, on the contrary, must believe it the same, especially when we remember the allusion to Seneca made by Polonius (Ham. II. 2). It may have been an earlier version, and probably was, *if there were no Globe theatre* before that opened in 1600 ; and if so, the reference to Seneca may have been a good-humoured retort to Nash's impertinence.

But Lord Campbell, having selected his text, proceeds to ignore it; and, taking up the pleadings of Mr. Collier, confines himself to the question, Was Shakespeare a lawyer's clerk before he became an actor? He does not go into the enquiry, Was the author of our 'Hamlet' a lawyer? Had he done so, he must certainly have given his verdict in the affirmative; because, when he comes to the soliloquy on the skull, beginning, "Where be his quiddits now?" (V. 1) he says:

These terms of art are all used, seemingly, with a full knowledge of their import. And it would puzzle some practising barristers with whom I am acquainted to go over the whole seriatim and define each of them satisfactorily (p. 89).

Instead of that, he limits himself to the issue raised by Collier, and sums up the evidence as it bears on that. He notices every passage which implies legal knowledge, and even refers to Shakespeare's last will and testament, as probably drawn by himself (p. 103); but he decides nothing, returning a verdict of "not proven."

"You require us," he says, "implicitly to believe a fact which, were it true, positive and irrefragable evidence in Shakspeare's own handwriting might have been forthcoming to establish. Though not enrolled as an attorney, it might have been reasonably expected that there would have been deeds or wills witnessed by him extant" (p. 111).

But he finds no evidence that Shakespeare had
been a lawyer, apart from the legal knowledge
discovered in the plays ; and he suggests that
it might have been picked up by listening to the
conversation of lawyers.

" Shakspeare," he remarks, " during his first years in
London, when his purse was low, may have dined at the
Ordinary in Alsatia, thus described by Dekker, where he
may have had a daily surfeit of law, if with his universal
thirst for knowledge he had any desire to drink deeply of
this muddy fountain : ' There is another ordinary at which
your London usurer, your stale bachelor, and your thrifty
attorney do resort, the price three pence, the rooms as full
of company as a gaol and indeed divided into wards like
the beds of an hospital. . . . If they chanced to discourse,
it is of nothing but statutes, bonds, recognizances, fines,
recoveries, audits, rents, subsidies, sureties, inclosures,
liveries, indictments, feoffments, judgments, commissions,
bankrupts, amercements and of such horrible matter ' (Gull's
Hornbook, 1609) " (p. 113).

In this, however, the judge is as inconsequential as Mr. Collier.   There is no better
proof that Shakespeare had a universal thirst for
knowledge, than that he was a lawyer ; both
conclusions are drawn from the materials of the
dramas ; and each is unconfirmed by independent evidence.   Thus, although a man might
pick up, in the way described, the legal know-

ledge displayed in 'Romeo and Juliet,' 'A Midsummer Night's Dream,' 'Love's Labour's Lost,' 'The Merchant of Venice,' 'Taming of the Shrew,' 'All's Well that ends Well,' 'The Winter's Tale,' 'Othello,' 'King John' and 'Henry VI.,' could he have thereby acquired what is shown in 'Hamlet,' which, as his Lordship allows, exceeded the capacity of "some practising barristers" of his acquaintance ? We must, nevertheless, take it from him that Shakespeare was not even a lawyer's clerk.

But, though he ignores Nash's testimony, we cannot do so. It may be unfavourable to William Shakespeare's claim ; but we are concerned only in establishing the truth about the plays ; and it is direct evidence, concerning the author of 'Hamlet.' It tells us that he was a lawyer; and that, in writing it, he had laid Seneca's tragedies under contribution. And both these statements are corroborated by the play. As Lord Campbell bears witness, it contains legal knowledge beyond some lawyers, and, therefore, as we may contend, beyond any layman.

It is, therefore, manifest that Shakespeare was not the author of ' Hamlet.'

We now pass on to the references in the
'Centurie of Prayse.' And the first is made by
Edmund Spenser, 1591, 'Colin Clout' (p. 1).

> And there, though last not least is Action,
> A gentle shepherd may nowhere be found
> Whose muse, full of high thoughts, invention,
> Doth, like himself, heroically sound.

The only authority for making this an
allusion to Shakespeare is the assumption that no
other name was heroical. The best proof that
Spenser did not refer to him is that, throughout
his works, he never mentions Shakespeare by
name, nor alludes either to his plays or poems.

The next refers to the play of 'Henry VI.' by
Thomas Nash, 1592, 'Pierce Penniless' (p. 5).

> How would it have joyed brave Talbot, the terror of the
> French, to think that after he had lain two hundred years
> in his tomb, he should so triumph again on the stage!

But here there is no word to indicate that
Nash recognized Shakespeare as the author.

What follows, however, is testimony in which
there is neither reticence nor ambiguity.

It is given by

Robert Greene, 'Groatsworth of Wit,' 1592
(p. 6).

There is an upstart crow, beautified with our feathers who, with his tiger's heart wrapped in a player's hide, supposes he is as well able to bombast out a blank verse, as the best of you, &c., being an absolute *Johannes Factotum*, is, in his own conceit, the only *Shake-scene* in a country.

This passage occurs in a letter, addressed to his "quondam associates," appended to the 'Groatsworth of Wit.' And we gather from it, that Greene and those, whom he addressed, had been in the habit of supplying Shakespeare with plays; but that he had now taken on himself to revise them; for bombasting out a blank verse can scarcely be understood as extending to the composition of an entire play.

During the two following years Shakespeare, nevertheless, published, as his own composition, the poems of 'Venus and Adonis' (1593), and 'The Rape of Lucrece' (1594), and dedicated them to the Earl of Southampton. Now dedications, in those days, not only inferred patronage, it was accepted as a certificate of merit and a title to popularity. The praise of Shakespeare, for as yet there had been none, accordingly begins next year, in an ode by

John Weaver, 'Ad Gulielmum Shakspeare,' 1595 (p. 16).

> Honey-tongued Shakspeare when I saw thine issue,
>   I swore Apollo got them and none other.
> Rose-cheeked Adonis with his amber tresses ;
>   Chaste Lucretia, virgin-like her dresses ;
> Proud, lust-stung Tarquin seeking still to prove her ;
> Romeo, Richard, *more whose names I know not*, &c.,

But Weaver was not only a bad poet, he was evidently unacquainted with literature and the drama, or he would at least have known the names of all the plays. He seems to have been a mere parasite of fortune, who rushed into print to hail the rising star.

The next references are in 1598, the first being taken from

Barnfield's Poems, 1598 (p. 26).

> And Shakspeare thou, whose honey-flowing vein,
> Pleasing the world, thy praises doth obtain,
> Whose Venus and whose Lucrece, pure and chaste,
> Thy name in Fame's immortal book have placed.

The second is from

Francis Meres, 1598, ' Palladis Tamia,' (C. of P., p. 21). The Italics are ours.

As Plåutus and Seneca are accounted the best of comedy and tragedy among the Latins,* so Shakespeare, among the

---

* Meres is evidently unaware that those of Seneca were the only Latin tragedies extant.

English, is the most excellent in both *for the stage*. For
comedy, witness his Two Gentlemen of Verona, his Errors,
his Love's Labour's Lost, his Love's Labour Won, his
Midsummer Night's Dream and his Merchant of Venice.
For Tragedy, his Richard II., Richard III., Henry VI.,
King John, Titus Andronicus and Romeo and Juliet.

But he adds:

These are our best for tragedy, Lord Buckhurst, Doctor
Leg(um) of Cambridge, Dr. Edes of Oxford, Master
Edward Ferris (Ferrers?), the author of The Mirror for
Magistrates, Marlowe, Peele, Watson, Kydd, Shakspeare,
Drayton, Chapman, Dekker, and Benjamin Jonson. The
best for comedy among us be Edward East of Oxford,
Master Rowley, once a rare scholar of learned Pembroke
Hall in Cambridge, Master Edwards, one of Her Majesty's
chapel, eloquent and witty John Lyly, Lodge, Gascoyne,
Greene, Shakspeare, Thomas Nash, Thomas Heywood,
Anthony Munday, our best plotter, Chapman, Porter,
Wilson, Hathaway and Henry Chettle.

And thirdly we have
Gabriel Harvey, 1598 (C. of P. p. 30).

The younger sort take much delight in Shakspeare's
Venus and Adonis; but the Lucrece and his tragedy of
Hamlet, Prince of Denmark, have it in them to please the
wiser sort.

Those are followed by

Henry Chettle, 1603, 'England's Mourning Garment' (C. of P. p. 55).

> Nor doth the silver-tonguéd Melicert
>   Drop from his mournful muse one sable tear
> To mourn her death who gracéd his desert.
>   And to his lays opened her royal ear—
> Shepherd, remember our Elizabeth,
>   And sing her rape done by that Tarquin, death.

Edmund Bolton, 1610, 'Hypercritica' (C. of P. p. 91).

The books out of which we gather the most warranted English are not many. . . . But among the chief, or rather the chief are in my opinion these:—Sir Thos. More's works, Geo. Chapman, first seven books of the Iliad, Samuel Daniel, Michael Drayton, his heroical epistles of England, Marlow, his excellent fragment of Hero and Leander, Shakspeare, Mr. Francis Beaumont and innumerable other writers for the stage and press tenderly to be used in this argument, Southwell, Parsons, and some few others of that sort.

John Davies, of Hereford, 1611, 'Scourge of Folly' (C. of P. p. 94).

> *To our English Terence, Mr. Will Shakespeare.*
> Some say, good Will, which I in sport do sing,
>   Hadst thou not played some kingly parts in sport,
> Thou hadst been a companion for a king,
>   And been a king among the meaner sort.

Thomas Freeman, 1614 (C. of·P. p. 106).

Shakspeare, that nimble Mercury, thy brain
    Lulls many hundred Argus eyes asleep ;
So fit for all thou fashionest thy vein,
    At the horse-foot fountain* thou hast drunk full deep.
Virtue's or vice's theme to thee all one is ;
    Who loves chaste life there's Lucrece for a teacher,
Who list read lust there's Venus and Adonis,
    True model of a most lascivious lecher,
Besides in plays thy wit winds like Meander,
    When needy new composers borrow more
Than Terence does from Plautus or Menander,
    But to praise thee aright I want thy store.
Then let thine own works thine own worth appraise
And help t' adorn thee with deservéd bays.

Of the above we may note that *Barnfield* and
Chettle limit their allusions to the poems ;
though the latter was acquainted with all the
theatrical gossip, going and had edited Greene's
' Groatsworth of Wit ; ' and, as regards *Francis
Meres*, the friend of Shakespeare, we cannot tell
whether he refers to Shakespeare as the author or
the proprietor of the plays, as Shakespeare undoubtedly was ; while *Harvey's* allusion to him

---

* Horse-foot fountain means Hippocrene, a fountain of Bœotia,
near Mount Helicon, the resort of the Muses. It was so called
because it sprang from the ground where Pegasus struck his feet,
and was therefore the fountain of the horse (ἵππος-κρήνη).

as the author of 'Hamlet,' and *Weaver's* as the
author of 'Romeo and Juliet,' are contradicted
respectively by our first quotation from Nash,
and the circumstances attending the publication
of the fourth 4to edition of 'Romeo and Juliet.'
Then *Bolton* only couples Beaumont's name with
plays, and *Davies* and *Freeman*, though apparently
acquainted with books, are not known as being
acquainted with the scandals of theatrical life.

Now these are all the allusions made to
Shakespeare during his life, though he was before
the public as an author for nearly a quarter of a
century; and, considering how many people
must have known him, it is marvellous they are
so few. Why have we nothing from Thomas
Kydd, George Peele, Thomas Lodge, George
Chapman, Samuel Daniel, Ben Jonson, Michael
Drayton, Christopher Marlowe, Thomas Dekker,
John Marston, John Fletcher, Francis Beaumont,
John Middleton or Philip Massinger? They
were all contemporaries, poets and dramatists;
and, if not all known as friends, must certainly
have been acquaintances. But the silence of
Philip Henslowe is even more remarkable.
Shakespeare and he, to a great extent, monopo-
lized the patronage of the play-going public—

were rival theatrical managers, perhaps open enemies, but assuredly keen-sighted acquaintances, who watched one another for almost twenty years. Yet, though Henslowe kept a diary which has come down to us, in which he noted all matters of interest, there is not a word about Shakespeare, good, bad, or indifferent. Indeed, for anything he has recorded, Mr. William Shakespeare may have been a myth. Now the silence of these people strikes us as far more surprising than that of the greater personages to whom Dr. Ingleby refers.

But it may be suggested that, perhaps, Shakespeare was noticed without being named, as is often the case now. There were doubtless many lampoons then; for more than a few are extant, and he may have been their subject as well as another. And so, Ben Jonson's sonnet on Poet-Ape, may be a case in point. At any rate we will give the reader an opportunity of forming an opinion by transcribing it. The italics are ours.

> Poor Poet-Ape, that would be thought our chief,
> 　Whose works are e'en the frippery of wit,
> From *brokage* is become so bold a thief
> 　As we, the robbed, leave rage and pity it.

At first he made low shifts, would pick and glean,
Buy the reversion of old plays. Now grown
To a little wealth and credit in the scene,
He takes up all, makes each man's wit his own,
And told of this, he slights it. Tut! such crimes
The sluggish, gaping auditor devours,
He marks not whose 'twas first, and after times
Many judge it to be his, as well as ours.
Fool! as if half-eyes will not know a fleece
From locks of wool and shreds from the whole piece.
                    (Gifford's Ben Jonson, III. 235)

This is really a paraphrase of Greene's Complaint. And, though Ben Jonson may not have been one of Greene's friends, he knew all about the 'Groatsworth of Wit'; for, in his comedy of the 'Silent Woman,' we read. "And one of them, I know not which, was cured with the Sick Man's Salve (religious tract, 1591), and the other with Greene's Groatsworth of Wit" (Jonson's Works, IV. 2). And, if the epigram do not apply to Shakespeare, we do not know to whom it can apply. It cannot be meant, as has been suggested, either for Marston, or Dekker, though Jonson quarrelled with both, because neither of them "grew to a little wealth," as Shakespeare did very soon. It must therefore, we think, be said, that Dr. Ingleby has omitted from his

'Centurie of Prayse,' one of the most important
allusions in contemporary authors. Gifford does
not suggest the time at which Jonson's epigrams
were written ; but we may fairly assume that this
was composed before 1598, when success had not
yet dawned on him ; and when, as we shall
hereafter see, his friendship with William
Shakespeare had not commenced.

CHAPTER XIII.

AUTHORSHIP OF THE PLAYS, CONTINUED.

Ben Jonson's Testimony.

WE now come to the well-known evidence of Ben Jonson, that, in fact, which has been put forward as an answer to all objectors to Shakespeare's authorship, and which is prefixed to the Folio of 1623. And first, we have the lines set opposite the portrait of the presumed author.

To the Reader.

This figure, that thou here see'st put, ·
It was for gentle Shakespeare cut,
Wherein the Graver had a strife
With Nature to out-doe the life.
Oh, could he but have drawne his wit,
As well in brasse, as he hath hit
His face ; the print would then surpasse
All that was ever writ in brasse.
But since he cannot, Reader, looke
Not on his Picture but his Booke.—B. J.

It would be unfair to found any conclusion on an engraving made in the beginning of the

seventeenth century ; but we cannot help re-
marking that the portrait is no more like the
Chandos portrait of Shakespeare, than it is like
Queen Elizabeth, perhaps not so much.

Then come the famous verses addressed

To the memory of my beloued,

THE AUTHOR,

MR. WILLIAM SHAKESPEARE

And

what he hath left vs.

To draw no enuy, (Shakespeare), on thy name
Am I thus ample to thy Booke and fame :
While I confesse thy writings to be such
As neither Man nor Muse can praise too much.
5 'Tis true, and all men's suffrage. But these wayes
Were not the paths I meant vnto thy praise :
For scaliest Ignorance on these may light,
Which, when it sounds at best, but echos right,
Or blinde Affection, which doth ne're aduance
10 The truth, but gropes, and vrgeth all by chance ;
Or crafty Malice, might pretend this praise,
And thinke to ruine where it seem'd to raise.
These are, as some infamous Baud or Whore
Should praise a Matron. What could hurt her more
15 But thou art proofe against them, and indeed
Aboue th' ill fortune of them, or the need.
I, therefore will begin. Soule of the age !
The applause ! delight ! the wonder of our Stage !
My Shakespeare, rise ; I will not lodge thee by

20 CHAUCER, or SPENSER, or bid BEAUMONT lye
    A little further, to make thee a roome :
  . Thou art a Moniment without a tombe,
    And art aliue still, while thy Book doth liue
    And we haue wits to read, and praise to giue.
25 That I not mixe thee so, my braine excuses ;
    I meane with great, but disproportion'd Muses :
    For, if I thought my iudgement were of yeeres,
    I should commit thee surely with thy peeres,
    And tell, how farre thou didst our LILY out-shine,
30 Or sporting KIDD or MARLOWES mighty line.
    And though thou hadst small Latine and lesse Greeke,
    From thence to honour thee, I would not seeke
    For names ; but call forth thund'ring Æschilus,
    Euripides, and Sophocles to vs,
35 Paccuus, Accius, him of Cordoua dead,
    To life againe, to heare thy Buskin tread,
    And shake a Stage : Or, when thy Sockes were on,
    Leaue thee alone, for the comparison
    Of all, that insolent GREECE or haughtie ROME
40 Sent forth, or, since did from their ashes come
    Triumph, my Britaine, thou hast one to showe,
    To whom all Scenes of EUROPE homage owe.
    He was not of an age, but for all time !
    And all the MUSES still were in their prime,
45 When like APOLLO, he came forth to warme
    Our eares, or like a MERCURY to charm !
    Nature herselfe was proud of his designes,
    And ioy'd to weare the dressing of his lines !
    Which were so richly spun, and wouen so fit,
50 As, since, she will vouchsafe no other Wit.
    The merry GREEKE tart ARISTOPHANES,
    Neat TERENCE, witty PLAUTUS now not please ;

But antiquated, and deserted lye
As they were not of Natures family.
55 Yet must I not giue Nature all : Thy Art,
My gentle Shakespeare, must enioy a part.
For though the Poets matter, Nature be,
His Art doth giue the fashion. And, that he,
Who casts to write a liuing line, must sweat,
60 (Such as thine are), and strike the second heat
Vpon the Muses anuile, turne the same,
(And himself with it), that he thinkes to frame ;
Or for the lawrele, he may gaine a scorne,
For a good Poet's made, as well as borne.
65 And such wert thou. Looke how the fathers face
Liues in his issue, euen so, the race
Of Shakespeares minde and manners brightly shines
In his well torned and true filed lines,
In each of which, he seemes to shake a Lance,
70 As brandish't at the eyes of Ignorance.
Sweet Swan of Auon ! what a sight it were
To see thee in our waters yet appeare,
And make those flights, vpon the bankes of Thames,
That so did take Eliza, and our Iames !
75 But stay, I see thee in the Hemisphere
Aduanc'd and made a Constellation there !
Shine forth, thou starre of Poets, and with rage,
Or influence, chide, or cheere the drooping Stage ;
Which, since thy flight fro hence, hath mourn'd like
    night,
80 And despaires day, but for thy Volumes light.

                    BEN IONSON.

Now there can be no doubt that the reader
was, by this address, expected to receive William

Shakespeare the actor, as the author of the plays. In this respect, it differs from what Ben Jonson says of Shakespeare in his ' Discoveries.' In heading that article he does not write *De Gulielmo Shakespeare*, " concerning William Shakespeare," but *De Shakespeare nostart* (*nostrate*) " concerning the Shakespeare of our country " whoever he might be. And it is quite possible that the word " Shakespeare " may have been used as a descriptive title, as appears from other circumstances besides its use in connection with the sonnets. If it be true that there was an alliance between the Italian and our stage, as shown in Chapter VII. there may have been an adoption of names from one to the other. Now as Isaac D'Israeli has pointed out, in his ' Curiosities of Literature' (article on pantomimic characters), the Italian pantomime actors had a *capitan*, called sometimes *Spavento* (Horrid Fright), and sometimes *Spizza-fer* (Shiver-spear). May not the wits of the time, who had been initiated into the theatrical mysteries, have adopted the name of Shiverspeare or Shakespeare to designate the new dramatic master? This would account for Ben Jonson's writing " of the Shakespeare of our country," for the apparent contradiction on the title-page of the sonnets, and for Francis Meres' allusions to Shakespeare as the author of plays. But, be that as it may, the general public would not have known it, and Jonson undoubtedly aided the players in deceiving them. The only question is, Was Ben Jonson capable of a deception for the sake of putting money in his pocket? To answer that we will briefly sketch the incidents of his previous life, as they are recorded by his biographer, Gifford.

He was born in 1573, being the posthumous son of a preacher, who had been ruined by his advocacy of the Reformation. By the favour of William Camden, at that time second master, he was educated at Westminster School (III. 481); but the circumstances of his family seemed to destine him to obscurity. His 'mother had married a bricklayer; and when he left school he had no other choice but to follow the same occupation; so that when he became disgusted with it, his only resource was to enlist in the army, then serving in the Low Countries. Returning thence, he seems to have followed the example of other poor scholars, and applied himself to literature, though apparently with less success than others, as he appears to have con-

tinued working at his trade. But in 1598, an
event occurred which, though it promised disas-
ter, led eventually to better fortune. On the
22nd of September in that year, he fought a
duel with one Gabriel Spencer, an actor in
Henslowe's company, whom he left dead on the
field.* While he lay in prison on that charge,
he was visited by a Catholic priest, who persuaded him to renounce Protestantism. Being
brought to trial in the following October, he
escaped by pleading "his clergy," and was then
introduced to Shakespeare, himself a papist, who
brought out Jonson's comedy of 'Every Man in
his Humour.'

Now any honest man might have changed his
religion on conviction; but Jonson told Sir
William Drummond that he was not convinced,
but he "took the priest's word for it" (III.
482). But why should he, unless the priest had
promised him the advantages he subsequently

---

* If ever an actor, Jonson was not one at the time of his duel,
for Henslowe, when writing to Alleyne on the subject, says, " Since
you were with me I have lost one of my company which hurteth
me greatly—that is Gabrell, for he is slain in Hogsden Fields by
the hands of Benjamin Jonson, bricklayer—therefore I would fain
have a little of your counsel," Sept. 26, 1598. (*Collier's Life of
Alleyne.*)

obtained? If so, what are we to say of the man who could act in such a way? Would he be a stickler for truth?

But worse follows. For twelve years, that is, from 1598 to 1610, Jonson remained a Catholic; yet, during that time, we find him acting as a spy on his co-religionists, and trying to find out which of them could be implicated in the Gunpowder Plot. Now the Gunpowder Plot justified the government in adopting any means to bring the conspirators to justice; but no honest man ever took up the business of espionage under any pretence, least of all under such circumstances as those which attended his treachery. Gifford, it is true, omits this episode from the life of his hero; but there can be no doubt of the fact; for here is his letter addressed to Lord Salisbury, and published in the 'Calendar of State Papers—Domestic Series—Reign of James I., 1603 to 1610, London, 1857.'

My most Honourable Lord, may it please your Lordship to understand there has been no want in me, either of labour or sincerity, in the discharge of this business, to the satisfaction of your Lordship and the State. And whereas yesterday, upon the first mention of it, I took the most ready course, to my present thought, by the Venetian

ambassador's chaplain, who not only apprehended it well,
but was of mind with me, *that no man of conscience or any
indifferent love to his country would deny to do it*, and
withal engaged himself to find out one absolute in all
numbers for the purpose, which he willed me, before the
gentleman of good credit who is my testimony, to signify .
unto your Lordship in his name.   It falls out since that
that party shall not be found ; for so he returns answer,
upon which I have made attempt in other places, but can
speak with no one in person, all being either removed or
concealed upon this present mischief.   But by second
means I have received answers of doubts and difficulties,
that they will make it a question to the arch-priest, with
other suchlike suspensions ; so that to tell your Lordship
plainly my heart, I think they are all so enweaved in it,
as it will make 500 gentlemen less of the religion within
this week, if they carry their understanding about them.
For myself, if I had been a priest, I would have put on
wings to such an occasion and have thought it no adventure,
*where I might have done, besides His Majesty and my
country, all Christianity so good service.*   And so much I
have sent to some of them.   If it shall please your
Lordship, I shall yet make further trial, and that you
cannot in the meantime be provided, I do not only with
all readiness offer my service, but will perform it with as
much integrity as your particular favour or his Majesty's
right in any subject he hath can exact.   Your Honour's
most perfect servant and lover,   BEN JONSON.

The reader will see from the words we have
put in italics, that Jonson was perfectly conscious of the business of the part he was playing,

and tried to excuse it under the pretence of patriotism ; but no man is required to sacrifice his honour to patriotism, though he may be required to sacrifice everything else.*

It will, perhaps, be said that he did not betray his co-religionists—that he only told Lord Salisbury what the Italian priest permitted him to say; but, if so, his treachery only changed its object. He betrayed his king and his country. On the assumption, however, that he was a loyal subject, he became the favourite of the Court, and was made poet-laureate ; while the Protestant authorities of the City of London appointed him to a lucrative office.

His chameleonesque religion was, nevertheless, destined to undergo another change. In 1610 he abjured popery, marking the sincerity of his recantation, as he informed Sir William Drummond, by emptying the cup at his communion, (III. 483). We are not told that he utilized his

---

* If Jonson could have foreseen that his letter to Lord Salisbury would one day be published, would he not have expunged No. 59 from his collection of epigrams ?

59.—On Spies.

Spies, you are lights in state but of base stuff,
Who, when you've burnt yourselves down to the snuff,
Stink and are thrown away—end fair enough.

re-conversion by becoming a Catholic spy on the
Protestant government, that trusted him ; we
know, however, that Jonson continued the friend
of Shakespeare as long as that actor lived.

But, whatever friendship existed between
them, Jonson could scarcely have had a very high
opinion of Shakespeare's genius, since a quarter
of a century passed (1598–1623) before he pens
a single line in his praise.   And, when, at last,
the laudatory verses do appear, we are sure he
was paid for writing them.   His testimony is
not, therefore, a spontaneous expression of his
own sentiments, but a business advertisement.
But we cannot help seeing what the players
were, of course, too ignorant to see—a half-
suppressed protest against what he felt obliged
to say.   Thus, having stated that the " Soul of
the age" had small Latin and less Greek, he
goes on to name the classic authors which had
inspired the plays, viz., Æschylus, to whose
' Agamemnon ' ' Macbeth ' was so much indebted ;
Euripides, whose ' Iphigeneia in Aulide ' had furnished the grand scene between Brutus and
Cassius in ' Julius Cæsar ; ' Sophocles, whose
' Electra ' had provided the model of ' Hamlet ; '
Pacuvius, to whose fragments ' King Lear ' owed

so much ; Accius (Plautus), the genius of all the comedies ; and " him - of Cordova " (Seneca), the type of the tragedies. Such cryptogrammatic evidence does not, however, atone for the open misleading of the public. And it would be idle to suppose that he was himself mislead. Whatever William Shakespeare may have pretended to be, Jonson knew him intimately and could not have been deceived.

But if Ben Jonson were salving his conscience with mental reservation when he wrote his address to " the memory of my beloved master," there was nothing in it, as Miss Delia Bacon has pointed out, except the words " Mr. William Shakespeare," that would not have applied to Francis Bacon. He also might be called the " Sweet swan of Avon," for the Avon flows by Cheltenham, where his great estate was, as well as by Stratford. And if William Shakespeare were literally dead in 1623, he also was dead to the world, having been disgraced and driven into retirement in 1621. Then the " small Latin and less Greek " might, to Jonson's vanity, appear enough for the great philosopher, though it would evidently be too much for William Shakespeare, whom all his contemporaries certify to have been entirely without art, *i.e.* without education. And lastly, he uses the same expressions to describe the works of Bacon and Shakespeare. Thus he said, of Bacon, in his 'Discoveries,' that—

He hath filled up all numbers and performed that in our tongue which may be *compared or preferred to insolent Greece or haughty Rome;* so that he may be named or stand as the mark and ἀκμή of our language.

while in this address we have—

Or, when thy socks were on,
Leave thee alone for thy comparison
Of all that insolent Greece or haughty Rome
Sent forth or since did from their ashes come.

CHAPTER XIV.

AUTHORSHIP OF THE PLAYS, CONTINUED.

Shakespeare's Personal Character—Aubrey MSS.—Manningham's Diary—Ward's MSS.—The Bidford Sippers —'Groatsworth of Wit'—Return from Parnassus No. 3—'Pierce Penniless'—'Ratsie's Ghost'—'Use of Richard II.' by Lord Essex—Lord Southampton's gift to Shakespeare—Signature of Shakespeare.

HAVING shown that the contemporaries of William Shakespeare previous to 1623 had no very exalted opinion of his genius, we will now inquire what historical evidence says of his personal character.

Of his early life very little is actually known. Rowe, his first biographer, writing from the information of Betterton, the player, who had gone to Stratford for the purpose of collecting evidence, tells us that he was the son of a leading burgess of that town. But all Betterton had found in the Stratford register was a statement that a certain John Shakespeare had a son, christened William, born in 1564. But Shakespeare was then and still is a common patronymic of the neighbourhood, so that a score of different children may have had the same name. The only scrap of real evidence is traditional, being contained in the *Aubrey* MSS., 1680 (C. of P., p. 383) which were not written till sixty-four years after his death. Aubrey says :

Mr. William Shakespeare was born at Stratford-upon-Avon, in the county of Warwick. His father was a butcher ; and I have been told heretofore by some of his neighbours that, *when he was a boy, he exercised his father's trade.* But, when he killed a calf, he would do it in a high style and make a speech. . . . This William, being inclined to poetry and acting, came to London, I guess about *eighteen* (1582 ?) and was an actor at one of the play-houses and did act exceedingly well. Now Ben Jonson was never a good actor, but an excellent instructor. He began early to make essays in dramatic poetry, which at that time was very low ; and his plays took well. He was a handsome, well-shaped man, very good company and of a very ready and pleasant, smooth wit. The humour of the constable in a 'Midsummer Night's Dream' (?) he happened to take at Grendon in Bucks, which is the road from London to Stratford ; and there was living that constable about 1642, when I first came to Oxon. Mr. Jos. Howe is of that parish, and knew him. Ben Jonson and he did gather humours of men daily, wherever they came. One time, as he was at the tavern at Stratford-upon-Avon, one Coombes an old rich usurer was to be buried. He makes there this extemporary epitaph :

Ten in the hundred the devil allows,
But Coombe will have twelve he swears and he vows.
If any one asks, " Who lies in this tomb?"
" Hoh ! " quoth the devil, " 'tis Jack o' Coombe." (*)

He was wont to go to his country once a year. I think I have been told he left 200 or 300 li. per annum, there and thereabout, to his sister. I have heard Sir William Davenant and Mr. Thomas Shadwell, who is counted the best comedian we have now, say, that he had a most prodigious wit and did admire his natural parts beyond all other dramatical writers. He was wont to say that he never blotted out a line. Said Ben Jonson " I wish he had blotted out a thousand." His comedies will remain wit as long as the English tongue is understood; for that he handles *mores hominum*. (Now our present writers reflect so much upon particular persons and coxcombites that twenty years hence they will not be understood.) Though, as Ben Jonson says, he had but little Latin and less Greek he understood Latin pretty well; for he had been, in his

* This impromptu was evidently a matter of common notoriety in Stratford, when Betterton visited the town, for Rowe gives it in his memoir of Shakespeare. He, however, alters it as follows—

Ten in the hundred lies here ingraved,
'Tis a hundred to ten his soul is not saved;
If any man ask, " Who lies in this tomb?"
" Oh! oh!" quoth the devil, " 'tis my John o' Coombe."

He thus not only improves the poetry, he relieves Shakespeare of the odium of having likened the Queen, his good patroness, to the enemy of souls. And it is undeniable that she had raised the legal rate of interest to ten per cent. ; for, though it were effected by Act of Parliament, no act was passed in her reign without her real assent. We also learn from Halliwell-Phillips' outlines, that Shakespeare himself was not above receiving it, though his church called it usury.

younger years, a schoolmaster in the country. Shakespeare
died a papist.

There is some contradiction in this statement;
because if "when he was a boy he exercised his
father's trade" of butchering, and went to
London "about eighteen," no time was left in
which he could have been "a schoolmaster in
the country." Otherwise the account is consistent enough with our experience of stage-
struck youth in later times; viz., a low origin,
and a flighty disposition, disdaining the mono-
tony of laborious occupation. But, if we take
his impromptu epitaph as a specimen, there is
no indication of either genius or education at a
time when he had attained mature age; for as
both John and William Combe, were alive in
1602, as will hereafter be shown, he would have
been thirty-eight at least.

Then we have evidence of a grossly animal
disposition.

In the diary of *John Manningham*, 1602
(C. of P., p. 45), we are told that

Upon a time when Burbage played Richard III.,
there was a citizen who had gone so far in liking him, that,
before she went from the play, she appointed him to come
that night unto her, by the name of Richard III.

Shakespeare, overhearing their conclusion, went before, was entertained and at his game, ere Burbage came. Then, message being brought that Richard III. was at the door, Shakespeare caused return to be made, that William the Conqueror was before Richard III. Shakespeare's name was William.

Nor was this a folly committed in the heyday of youth. Richard Burbage did not make his appearance till 1603; so that Shakespeare must have been forty, if not more.

Then we have the testimony of *John Ward*, the vicar of Stratford, contained in MSS. covering the period embraced by 1648 and 1679 (C. of P., p. 327). He says:

> Shakespeare was a natural wit, *without any art at all.* He frequented the plays all his younger time, but in his elder days lived at Stratford and supplied the stage with two plays every year; and for that he had an allowance so great, that he spent at the rate of a thousand a year, as I have heard.

>   *   *   *   *

> Shakespeare, Drayton, and Ben Jonson had a merry meeting and, it seems, drank too hard; for Shakespeare died of a fever there contracted (delirium tremens).

Another memorial is given by Mr. Halliwell Phillips, who has thought proper to preserve the MS. containing the account. From that it appears that a party at Bidford, a village six miles from Stratford, went by the name of "the Bidford topers," and being proud of their power of drinking challenged Shakespeare and his boon companions to a trial of strength. When, however, they arrived at Bidford, the topers had gone to Evesham fair; so they accepted an invitation from certain persons, who called themselves "the sippers." But they were not destined to be victorious. Having become intoxicated, they gave up the contest and set out to their return home. Half a mile from Bidford was, nevertheless, as near as they got to Stratford. They lay down under a crab-tree beside the road, and slept till morning. They were roused from their slumbers by their late antagonists, who invited them to return to Bidford and renew the contest. Shakespeare, in refusing, took occasion to vaunt his own prowess; while he uttered that charming quatrain, which still enchants the world. I have drunk, he said, with

Piping Pepworth, dancing Marston,
Haunted Hillborough, hungry Grafton,
Dodging Exhull, papist Wicksford,
Beggarly Brown, and drunken Bidford.(*)

* Another impromptu, preserved in the Ashmole MSS., No. 38, has been ascribed to him—

Mr. Phillips thinks that "the whole story, when viewed strictly with reference to the habits and opinions of those days, presents no features that suggest disgrace to the principal actor, or imposition on the part of the narrator." And he adds that some foundation for the tale may be gathered from the fact that "as late as 1762, the tree, then known as 'Shakespeare's canopy' was regarded at Stratford-on-Avon as an object of great interest" ('Outlines of Shakespeare's Life').

But if the foregoing be merely tradition, we have the evidence of a contemporary, to whom we have already referred, Robert Greene, who seems to have known the man to his own bitter cost.

In his 'Groatsworth of Wit'—we quote from the facsimile reprint, published by the Shakespeare Society in what are called the

---

"Mr. Ben Jonson and Mr. Wm. Shakespeare being at a tavern, Mr. Jonson began this for his epitaph—

"Here lies Ben Jonson
Who was once one——"

And gives it Mr. Shakespeare to make up, who presently writ—

"That while he lived was a slow thing,
And now being dead is no-thing."

Allusion   Books—we   have   the   following
letter :

> To those gentlemen, his quondam acquaintances that
> spend their wits in making plays, R. G. wisheth a better
> exercise and wisdom to prevent his extremities.

The persons thus indicated have been identified as (1) Christopher Marlowe; (2) Thomas
Nash ; and (3) George Peele. The italics are
ours.

> If woeful experience may move you, gentlemen, to
> beware, or unheard of miseries intreat you to take heed, I
> doubt not but you will look back with sorrow on your time
> past and endeavour with repentance to spend that which is
> to come.   Wonder not—for with thee I will begin—thou
> famous gracer of tragedians (Marlowe) that Greene, who
> hath said with thee like the fool in his heart, there is no
> God, should now give glory unto his greatness; for
> penetrating is his power ; his hand lies heavily upon me ;
> he hath spoken unto me with a voice of thunder; and I
> have felt that he is a GOD that can punish enemies. Why
> should thy excellent wit, his gift, be so blinded that thou
> shouldst give no glory to the giver ?   Is it pestilent Machia-
> vellian policy that thou hast studied ?   Oh ! punish folly !
> What, are his rules but mere confused mockeries, able to
> extirpate in small time the generation of mankind ? For,
> if *sic volo, sic jubeo* hold in those that are able to command,
> and if it be lawful *fas et nefas* to do anything that is
> beneficial, only tyrants should possess the earth ; and they
> striving to exceed in tyranny, should each to other be a

slaughterman, till the mightiest outliving all, one stroke were left for death, that, in our age, man's life should end. The brother of this diabolical atheism is dead and never in his life had the felicity he aimed at; but as he began in craft, lived in fear and died in despair *quàm inscrutabilia sunt dei justicia !* This murderer of many brethren had his conscience seared like Cain; this betrayer of him that gave his life for him, inherited the portion of Judas; this apostate perished as ill as Julian.   And wilt thou, my friend, be his disciple? Look unto me, by him persuaded to that liberty; and thou shalt find it an infernal bondage. I know the least of my demerits merits this miserable death; but wilful striving against known truth exceedeth all the terrors of my soul.   Defer not with me till this last point of extremity; for little knowest thou how in the end thou shalt be visited.

With thee I join young Juvenal (Thomas Nash) that biting satirist, that lately with me together writ a comedy. Sweet boy, might I advise thee, be advised and get not many enemies by bitter words.   Inveigh against vain men, for thou canst do it, no man better, no man so well.   Thou hast a liberty to reprove all and name none; for once being spoken to, all are offended; none being blamed, no man is injured.   Stop shallow water still running, it will rage; tread on a worm, it will turn.   Then blame not scholars, vexed with sharp lines, if they reprove thy too much liberty of reproof.

And thou (Peele) no less deserving than the other two, in some things rarer, in nothing inferior, driven like myself to extreme shifts, a little have I to say to thee.   And, were it not an idolatrous oath, I would swear by sweet St. George, thou art unworthy better hap sith thou dependest on so mean a stay.   Base-minded men all three of you, if, by my misery, ye be not warned ; *for unto none of you, like me, sought those burrs to cleave—those puppets I mean that speak from our mouths, those antics, garnished in our colours.* Is it not strange that I, to whom they all have been beholden——is it not like that you, to whom they all have been beholden, shall, were ye in that case that I am now, be both at once of them forsaken? Yes, trust them not ; for *there is an upstart crow beautified with our feathers, that, with his tiger's heart wrapped in a player's hide, supposes he is as well able to bombast out a blank verse as the best of you, and being an absolute Johannes factotum is, in his own conceit, the only Shake-scene in a country.* O, that I might extract your rare wits to be employed in more profitable courses ; and let these apes imitate your past excellence and never more acquaint them with your admired inventions. I know the best husband of you all will never prove an usurer ; and the kindest of them all will never prove a kind nurse. Yet, whilst you may, seek you better masters ; for it is pity men of such rare wits should be subject to the pleasure of such rude grooms.

In this I might *insert two others* that both have writ against these *buckram gentlemen ;* but let their own marks serve to witness against their own wickedness, if they persevere to maintain any more such peasants. For *other new comers,* I leave them to the mercy of those painted monsters, who, I doubt not, will drive the best-minded to despise them. For the rest, it skills not, though they make a jest at them.

But now return I again to you three, knowing my misery is to you no news, and let me earnestly entreat you to be warned by my harms. Delight not, as I have done, in irreligious oaths ; for from the blasphemer's house a curse

shall not depart. Despise; drunkenness which wasteth the
wit, making men all equal unto beasts. Fly lust as the
deathsman of the soul and defile not the temple of the Holy
Ghost. *Abhor those epicures, whose loose life* hath made
religion loathsome in your ears ; and when they soothe you
with terms of mastership, (*) remember, Robert Greene,
whom they have often so flattered, perishes now for want
of comfort. Remember, gentlemen, your lives are like so
many lighted tapers, that are with care delivered to you.
Then with wind-puffed works may be extinguished, with
drunkenness put out, with negligence let fall ; for man's
time is not so short but it is more shortened by sin. The
fire of my life is now at the last snuff and the want of
wherewith to sustain it. There is no substance left for life
to feed on. Trust not then, I beseech ye, to such weak
stays ; for they are as changeable in mind, as in many
attires. Well, my hand is tired and I am forced to leave
where I would begin ; for a whole book cannot contain
their wrongs, which I am forced to knit up in some few
lines of words. Desiring you should live, though himself be
dying,

ROBERT GREENE.

In this letter William Shakespeare received a
character which can scarcely be deemed consistent with a divinely-inspired genius. We
say nothing of the loose life which ruined the
morals of his associates. But he is a mere Jack-
of-all-trades—a man with a tiger's heart, who

* In those days Masters of Arts were formally addressed as
Master, and Bachelors of Arts, *Sir*.

would allure scholars to do his work, fawn on
them, suck their brains, and cast them off when
they had served his turn—while, for we cannot
omit this, he would represent to the world that
their works were his own.   And whatever
special pleading may advance to the contrary,
" an upstart now beautified with our feathers "
means that, or it means nothing.   It could not
refer to his being an actor, because an actor
makes no false pretence ; and false pretence is
the essence of the fable of the " Crow in
Peacock's feathers," which he chooses for his
allegory.   But the worshippers of Shakespeare
have taken such pains to discredit Greene's
evidence, that we shall pause to consider its
credibility.

Robert Greene, according to Dr. Ingleby's introduction to the ' Groatsworth of Wit,' was born at
Norwich in 1560, and entered St. John's College,
Cambridge, 1574–5 (?).   He took his A.B. 1578,
and A.M. 1583, having exchanged from St.
John's College to Clare Hall before proceeding
to the latter.   After leaving the University, he
travelled in Spain and Italy, and, according to
his own showing, was guilty of much extrava-
gance.   In 1584, however, he took orders, and

was appointed Vicar of Tollesbury, Essex, and about the same time commenced the study of medicine. In 1586 he married, and two years later was incorporated at Oxford. In spite, therefore, of any indiscretions abroad, his character, thus far, was of fairly good repute. The rest of his story, which covers only a space of four years, may be gathered from the 'Groatsworth of Wit,' for at the close of that he says :

> Here, gentlemen, break I off Roberto's speech, whose life, in most parts agreeing with mine, found one self-punishment (p. 26).

And from the 'Groatsworth of Wit' we learn that Robert, having been disinherited by his father, was at last driven to write for the players, whose dissolute society completed his ruin. We do not know how Greene's clerical preferment was lost. We may infer it was not for his good conduct. What we do know is that his wife abandoned him, leaving their only child on his hands ; the pathetic letter in which he implores for compassion for the unhappy infant being appended to the tale in question.

Now it was practically from his deathbed this,

N

Greene's last book, was published.*   Thus, in
the letter of Henry Chettle, prefixed to ' Kind-
heart's Dream,' we read :

About three months since died Mr. Robert Greene,
leaving many papers in sundry booksellers' hands.   Among
others his Groatsworth of Wit, in which a letter, written
to diverse play-makers, is offensively by one or two of them
taken.

He then refers to a report that either Mr.
Thomas Nash or he was the author of it, which

---

* The facsimile reprinted by the New Shakspeare Society is not
that of the first edition, 1592, but that of 1596.   The full title of
the book is as follows :

GREENE'S

GROATSWORTH OF WIT.

BOUGHT WITH A MILLION OF

REPENTANCE.

Describing the folly of youth, the falsehood of make-shift
flatterers, the misery of the negligent, and mischiefs
of deceiving . . . . . Courtezans.

WRITTEN BEFORE HIS DEATH AND PUBLISHED AT HIS
DYING REQUEST.

Fælicem fuisse infaustum.

LONDON:

PRINTED BY THOMAS CREDE FOR RICHARD OLIVE
DWELLING IN LONG LANE; AND ARE THERE
TO BE SOLD.
1596.

he denies in the most explicit manner. He admits having re-written Greene's MS. on account of its illegibility; but he adds that, though he had "struck something out," he had "not put a word in."

"With neither of them that take offence," he says, "was I acquainted, and with one of them, I care not if I never be. The other, whom, at that time, I did not so much spare, as since I wish I had; for that as I have moderated the heat of living writers and might have used my own discretion, especially in such a case, the author being dead. That I did not, I am as sorry, as if the original fault had been my fault; because myself have seen his demeanour no less civil, than he excellent in the quality he professes. Besides, diverse of worship have reported his uprightness of dealing, which argues his honesty; and his facetious grace in writing approves his heart." (See *Kind-heart's Dream—Shakespeare Allusion Books*, Series IV. part I. page 37.)

Now it would be immaterial, if we could prove, which of the four—Shakespeare, Marlowe, Nash, or Peele—was the one Chettle wished he had never spared. He offers no opinion of his. own on Greene's charge; so that for anything we see, it still stands intact. But where is the emphatic denial under the hand of Shakespeare? According to his admirers, he was a practised and very powerful writer.

Why was his pen idle? Was the charge too trivial for notice; or, like an astute man of the world, did he judge that the more he stirred, the more he would stink? Surely this is Poet-ape over again, who

> takes up all, makes each man's wit his own ;
> And *told of this, he slights it.*

Depend on it, we have at last found the date on which Ben Jonson's memorable epigram was written, as well as the name of the person on whom he wrote it.

But it may be said that Nash denies it. But Nash does nothing of the kind in the epistle prefixed to the second edition of 'Pierce Penniless,' on which the pretence for his denial is founded. His words are :

Other news I am advertised of—that a scald, trivial, lying pamphlet, called Greene's Groatsworth of Wit, is given out to be of my doing. God never have care of my soul, but utterly renounce me, if the least word or syllable in it proceeded from my pen, or if I were in any way privy to the writing or printing of it. (*Supplement to the Introduction to the Shakespeare Allusion Books*, Part I. page xliii.)

Now, as the writer of the Supplement informs us, Nash was at this time living in the house of

Archbishop Whitgift at Croydon.   He might, therefore, naturally resent being exposed as the companion and servant of the players, and denounce the pamphlet as "scald, trivial, and lying," but that would only mean so far as he was concerned.   He would deny nothing on behalf of Shakespeare.   As far, therefore, as we know, no one really takes up the cudgels against Greene, until Gabriel Harvey's third letter appears (1592).   But Harvey was notoriously the enemy of Greene, who, in spite of his own advice to Nash, had lampooned him and his astrological pretensions in " A Quip for an Upstart Courtier."   Yet what does Harvey find to say ?

Greene, vile Greene, wouldst thou wert half so honest as the worst of the four thou upbraidest. (*Shakespeare Allusion Books*, Series IV. part I. p. 130.)

This, no doubt, asserts that Greene had been a very bad man—a fact the poor fellow had categorically admitted—but it does not refute his charge against Shakespeare.   Neither is the incriminated cleared by his assertion, that Greene, so far from having perished for want of comfort, had died of a surfeit of pickled

herrings and Rhenish wine. Indeed all he
says of him seems to have been attributed to
malice by contemporaries. Thus Francis Meres
says :

As Achilles tortured the dead body of Hector, and as
Antonius and his wife, Fulvia, tormented the lifeless corpse
of Cicero ; so Gabriel Harvey showed the same inhumanity
to Greene that lies full low in his grave. (*Palladis Tamia*,
1598—*Shakespeare Allusion Books* —Series IV. p. 164.)

The charge, in fact, remains unrefuted to the
present hour, the admirers of Shakespeare being
driven to shelter him under a denial of Greene's
credibility.

But we must not disbelieve him because he
had been a bad man. He could have had no
inducement to die with a lie in his mouth. On
the contrary the circumstances of the case would
lead him to speak nothing but the truth. He
was addressing men who knew Shakespeare as
well as he did ; and he is referring to their
plays as much as to his own. If he said what
they knew to be false, he might just as well
have held his tongue. Then, if we give effect to
our own rule of law, which admits, as good
evidence, the testimony of a man who believes

himself to be dying, we must admit this
evidence against Shakespeare.

And similar evidence of the misery of those
who wrote for the players had before been
given.   Indeed, Greene may refer to such, when
he says of the two others, that they *both have
writ against these buckram gentlemen.*   Who they
were, or what they said, we do not know.   They
may have been the authors of the ' Pilgrimage
to Parnassus' and the ' Return from Parnassus ; '
because, though the first was not acted at St.
John's College till the Christmas of 1598, they
may have been written long before.   At any
rate, in the ' Return from Parnassus,' No. 3 of
the trilogy, we have this remarkable passage :

Fair fell good Orpheus, that would rather be
King of a mole-hill than a Keysar's slave.
Better it is 'mongst fiddlers to be chief
Than at a player's trencher beg relief.
But is't not strange those mimic apes should prize (?)
Unhappy scholars at a hireling's rate ? (?)
Vile world, that lifts them up to high degree,
But treads us down in grovelling misery.
England affords those glorious vagabonds,
That carried erst their fardels on their backs,
Coursers to ride on thro' the gazing streets,
Sooping it in their glaring satin suits,
And pages to attend their masterships.

With mouthing words that better wits have framed
They purchase lands and now esquires are made.
     (*Shakespeare Allusion Books*, Gen. Introd. p. iii.)

Again, in a pamphlet entitled 'Ratsie's Ghost,' the greed of players is set forth in the following advice given to an actor (C. of P. p. 67):

Get thee to London; for, if one man were dead (R. Burbage?), they will have much need of such a one as thou art. There would be none, in my opinion, fitter than thyself to play his parts. My conceit is such of thee, that I durst venture all the money in my purse on thy head to play Hamlet against him for a wager. There thou shalt learn to be frugal (for players were never so thrifty as they are now about London) *and to feed upon all men*, to make thy hand a stranger to thy pocket, thy heart slow to perform thy tongue's promises. And, when thou feelest thy purse well lined, buy thee some place or lordship in the country, that, growing weary of playing, thy money may bring thee to dignity and reputation.

This pamphlet is undated; but it is bound up with others of the years 1603 and 1604. As Shakespeare had begun to buy land at Stratford in 1602 (see Halliwell Phillipps, 'Outlines of the Life of Shakespeare,' London, 1886, I. 196), it is probable this is an allusion to him.

But the character of our bard receives a fresh colour. He now comes before us, a man as disloyal to the queen who had patronised him, as was consistent with his own safety. When the Earl of Essex, one of the most ungrateful scoundrels who ever breathed, was preparing for the insurrection which Lord Southampton and he attempted to raise, he employed one Dr. Hayward to write a pamphlet, suggesting an analogy between the queen and himself and Richard II. and Bolingbroke, and advising, that it was desirable she should be deposed, like Richard; and that he, like Bolingbroke, should be raised to the throne. The pamphlet having been extensively circulated, the tragedy of 'Richard II.' was repeatedly performed, the last performance taking place on the very eve of the rising (C. of P. p. 36). Now there was no treason in the play itself. It became treasonable only when connected with Hayward's commentary; and the Queen very properly held Essex responsible for it. Shakespeare, in spite of Mr. Donnelly's cryptogram, was evidently beneath her notice. Thus we read, in Nicholls' 'Progresses and Processions of Queen Elizabeth' (C. of P. p. 449), of

That which passed from the excellent Majesty of Q. Elizabeth, in her privy chamber at East Greenwich, 4th of

August, 1601, and 43rd year of her reign, to William
Lambard.

Lambard having presented his Pandecta of
the Rolls, the Queen's eye falls on the name of
' Richard II.,' when the following colloquy takes
place :

Q. Eliz. I am Richard II. Know ye not that ?

Lamb. Such a wicked imagination was determined by a
most unkind (unnatural) gentleman, the most
adorned creature that ever your Majesty made.

Q. Eliz. He that will forget God will also forget his
benefactor. This tragedy was played forty
times in open streets and houses.

Now if it were true that it was played in open
streets, and there is no reason for doubting
the Queen's word, Shakespeare must have known
why it was so played, and was, . therefore,
constructively as treacherous as Lord Essex
himself. But the incident throws a fresh light
on the story told by Rowe of Lord Southampton's generosity—a light which reveals a still
deeper stain on the character of our national
bard.

What grace soever, he says, the Queen bestowed upon
him (Shakespeare), it was not to her only he owed the

fortune, which the reputation of his wit made. He had the honour to meet with many great and uncommon marks of favour and friendship, from the Earl of Southampton, famous in the histories of that time, for his friendship to the unfortunate Earl of Essex. It was to that noble lord he dedicated his poem of ' Venus and Adonis.' There is one instance so singular in the munificence of this patron of Shakspeare's, that, if I had not been assured that the story was handed down by Sir William Davenant, who was probably very well acquainted with his affairs, I should not have ventured to have inserted, that my Lord Southampton, at one time gave him a thousand pounds, to enable him to go through with a purchase he had a mind to. A bounty very great and very rare at any time, and almost equal to that profuse generosity the present age has shown to French dancers and Italian singers. (*Rowe's Memoir*, p. viii.)

Considering the different value of money in those days, it was a greater bounty than any patron has been known to bestow on literary merit, at any time whatever. In fact, it seems utterly incredible, until we remember that Southampton was implicated in Essex's conspiracy, and was tried and convicted along with him, though he was subsequently pardoned. If, however, Shakespeare were in possession of information, which would have excluded Southampton from the leniency he found, it is easy to understand that Shakespeare was able to make

his own terms for keeping silence. And the
dates coincide with this hypothesis. Southampton was tried and convicted on the 19th of
February, 1601 ; but while Essex was brought
to the block six days after, Southampton's life
was spared; and he was finally set at liberty
by James I., on the 5th of April, 1603. Shakespeare began buying land 1602, and completed
the purchase of a moiety of the tithes of Stratford
in the summer of 1605.*

Nor are those minor details wanting, which
go so far to measure a man's true character.

Unlike Alleyne, Field, Burbage or Tarleton,
Shakespeare achieved no success in the profession he had chosen. Rowe says : " Though
I have enquired, I could never meet with any
further account of him this way, than that the
top of his performance was the Ghost in his
own 'Hamlet.' " (p. vi.) Certainly no such

---

* Mr. Halliwell Phillips, in his 'Outlines' (Vol. I., pp. 196–7),
reprints the indenture, dated May 1st, 1602, made between William
Coombe of Warwick and John Coombe of Stratford-upon-Avon,
and William Shakespeare, for the purchase of 107 acres of arable land
at the sum of £320. Also that for the purchase of a moiety of the
lease of the tithes of Stratford-upon-Avon, Old Stratford, Bishop-
ton, and Welcombe, dated July 24th, 1605, the consideration for
the same being the sum of £440. Here, then, would be £760 out
of the £1,000 given by Southampton.

eulogiums on his acting have reached us, as
those bestowed on the actors we have named.
If, therefore, we may judge by the result, conceit rather than genius led him to the stage.

Then, though some would have us believe
he was a professional writer, his signature is
entirely dissimilar to the signature of other
authors of his time ; such as Francis Bacon,
Camden, Raleigh, Ben Jonson, or, even to men
whose business required them to write, such
as Francis Collyns, his attorney, or Thomas
Quinsy, his son-in-law. All of them use large,
distinct characters for their names quite unlike
the small, connected letters of ordinary manu-
script ; while Shakespeare uses the common
script, as people unaccustomed to writing do
at the present time.

Again, though by repute a voluminous author,
not a scrap of his copy, nor so much as a
fragment of one of his letters has been discovered by a long-continued and exhaustive
search.   From what the players say of the
unblotted condition of the plays they received
from him, (see their address, prefixed to the
Folio of 1623) it is evident they never saw the
draft of any one of the plays. Indeed, for

anything that exists under his hand, or for anything we have heard to the contrary, his penmanship may only have extended to the feat of scrawling his name.

What we do learn, and that from his biographer and admirer, Mr. Halliwell Phillipps (Author of the ' Life of Shakespeare '), is, that he was a money-lender, who would have his pound of flesh at all hazards, and a keen man of business, who kept the main chance always before him ; while our other evidence shows he knew how to suck poor men's brains at a small expense. That he was a wit—a tavern wit— may be conceded ; that he was a man of grossly animal nature cannot be denied. But we have not a single instance recorded of friendship, kindness, or generosity.

Now it would be an insult to the reader's understanding to argue that he could not be the author of the plays ; and we shall not attempt to do so. How he became possessed of them is evident enough, and may be read in Ben Jonson's epigram on Poet-Ape.

CHAPTER XV.

AUTHORSHIP OF THE PLAYS, CONTINUED.

Authors suggested by the 'Groatsworth of Wit,' Greene,
Marlowe, Nash, and Peele.

FROM the 'Groatsworth of Wit' we learn
that plays produced by Shakespeare before 1592
were written by Greene, Marlowe, Nash, and
Peele. It also suggests " two more " and refers
also to " other new comers." At present,
however, we shall confine ourselves to the four
above named. They all, as we have seen,
belonged to the class of poor scholars, and were
just such persons as an unscrupulous man of
business would be likely to make use of. They
were popular writers, but poor and dissolute,
the very characters best suited to the purpose
of a man like Shakespeare. How little he gave
them for their work may be estimated by what
Ben Jonson said of his theatrical gains to
William Drummond, in 1618, when he had been

a successful dramatist for twenty years; viz.,
that he had not gained two hundred pounds by
all his plays (Jonson's Works, III. 490). But be
that as it may, if we had a chronology of the
production of Shakespeare's dramas we might put
our finger on the pieces written by them. But
we have no such chronology. All we know is
that, in 1589, Nash speaks of 'Hamlet' as
already produced; while, in 1598, Francis Meres
gives the list of plays as consisting of

'Richard II.,' 'Richard III.,' 'Henry IV.,' 'King John,'
'Titus Andronicus,' 'Romeo and Juliet,' 'Comedy of Errors,'
'Love's Labour's Lost,' 'Love's Labour Won,' 'Two Gentlemen of Verona,' 'Midsummer Night's Dream,' 'Merchant
of Venice.' (*Palladis Tamia*, p. 161.)

But 'Hamlet' must be left out.   It is in a style
totally different to that of any of our present
authors; whilst Meres' list contains one, 'Romeo
and Juliet,' which was quite beyond their
capacity. With these exceptions, we think, our
poor scholars equal to writing any of them, before
the plays had undergone, what most of them
doubtless did undergo, a more or less careful
revision. And that will not be difficult to show,
if we refer to their published works.

Greene was a voluminous author of plays, poems, romances and tracts, of which we may mention 'Orlando Furioso,' 'Alphonsus, King of Arragon,' 'James IV.,' 'A Looking-glass for London,' in conjunction with Lodge's 'Farewell to Folly' and the 'Groatsworth of Wit.' His writings, in all their forms, show a constant endeavour to exhibit learning even at the expense of consistency. Great indecency characterises some of his productions; while others are quite in the preaching vein. He is a decided euphuist, his rhetoric being laboriously antithetical and crowded with similes. His works were edited by Dyce in 1831.

The following may be taken as specimens of his style :—

Fair queen of love, thou mistress of delight,
Thou gladsome lamp that wait'st on Phœbe's train,
Spreading thy kindness thro' the jarring orbs
That, in their union, praise thy lasting power,
Thou, that hast stayed the fiery Phlegons course
And mad'st the coachman of the glorious wain
To droop in view of Daphne's excellence,
Fair pride of morn, sweet beauty of the ev'n,
Look on Orlando languishing in love.
                                        (*Orlando Furioso.*)

Sweet are the thoughts which savour of content,
The quiet mind is richer than a crown ;

O

Sweet are the nights in careless slumber spent,
  The poor estate scorns fortune's angry frown.
Such sweet content, such minds, such sleep, such bliss
Beggars enjoy when princes oft do miss.

                              (*Farewell to Folly.*)

Ah! what is love? It is a pretty thing,
As sweet unto a shepherd as a king,
        And sweeter too;
For kings have cares, that wait upon a crown,
And cares can make the sweetest things to frown.
        Ah! then, ah! then,
If country loves such sweet desires gain,
What lady would not love a shepherd swain?

                              (*Pair of Turtle Doves.*)

His prose style may be gathered from his
'Groatsworth of Wit,' already quoted.

What are his (Machiavelli's) rules but mere confused
mockeries, able to extirpate, in small time, the generation
of mankind? For if *sic volo, sic jubeo* hold in those that
are able to command, and if it be lawful *fas et nefas* to do
anything that is beneficial, only tyrants should possess the
earth; and they, striving to exceed in tyranny, should each
to other be a slaughterman, till, the mightiest outliving all,
one stroke were left for death, that, in one age, man's life
should end. The brother of this diabolical atheism is dead,
and never in his life had the felicity he aimed at; but, as
he began in craft, lived in fear and died in despair. *Quàm
inscrutabilia sunt dei judicia!* This murderer of many
brethren had his conscience seared like Cain; this betrayer

of him that gave his life for him, inherited the portion of Judas; this apostate perished as ill as Julian.

The pieces in Meres' list we should assign to him are *Love's Labour's Lost* and the *Comedy of Errors*.

Love's Labour's Lost is in his worst style—vulgar, childish, and indecent. In fact, it would be difficult to find a worse play, until we come to the days of 'The Two Noble Kinsmen.' In it he loses no opportunity of showing off his erudition, quoting Latin and Italian, using medical terms and having a turn at the gamut (IV. 2). Nay, he even makes some of his characters use false Latin, that he may show his learning in correcting it (V. 1); while he uses the same idea which we find in the 'Groatsworth of Wit,' that the lives of vain men are " like tapers " (V. 2). The songs introduced, however, are, with one exception, very pretty and quite worthy of his best lyrical efforts.

The Comedy of Errors, though adapted from such an excellent model, is tedious and uninteresting; but it is entirely in his style.

Marlowe, considering the shortness of his life, was a very prolific author. In addition to

anything he may have written for Shakespeare,
he wrote 'Tamburlaine' in three parts, 'The Jew
of Malta,' 'The Massacre of Paris,' 'Dido,' in
conjunction with Nash, and 'Edward II.' He
translated Ovid's 'Elegies,' and the first book
of 'Lucan,' leaving a fragment of 'Hero and
Leander,' an imitation, rather than a translation,
of the famous poem of Musæus.

In all his compositions we discover the characteristics of youthful genius. He is often
sublime, always spirited, but exuberant, im-
pulsive, and bombastic, and while his fondness
for detail, his habit of describing character,
instead of showing it in action, and of making
his villains confess themselves such—a practice
never observed in real life—unmistakably pro-
claim the novice. His tragedy, nevertheless,
contrasts very favourably with that of his
predecessors. His declamation is more animated
and natural, and, unlike theirs, is closely connected with the moving incidents of a bustling
drama. In other respects the characteristic of
his writing is the characteristic of his natural
disposition. It is grossly animal, and reveals, in
a greater degree than that of any other author of
his time, the φρόνημα τῆς σαρκὸς, or carnal mind.

The following extracts from his dramatic works will afford specimens of his style :

Unhappy Persia, that in former age
Hast been the seat of mighty conquerors,
That in their *prowess* and their *polices*
Have triumphed over Afric and the bounds
Of Europe, where the sun dares scarce appear
For freezing meteors and congealéd cold,
Now to be ruled and governed by a man
At whose birthday Cynthia with Saturn joined,
And Jove, the Sun and Mercury denied
To shed their influence on his fickle brain,
Now Turks and Tartars shake their swords at thee,
Meaning to mangle all thy provinces. (1 *Tamburlaine*, I. 1.)

Barabus to another Jew.

1*st Jew.* A fleet of warlike galleys, Barabus,
　　　　Are come from Turkey and lie in our roads ;
　　　　And they, this day, sit in the Council-house
　　　　To entertain them and their embassy.
Bara.　Why, let 'em come, so they come not to war
　　　　Or, let 'em war, so we be conquerors,
　　　　Nay, let 'em combat, conquer and slay all,
　　　　So they spare me, my daughter, and my wealth.
　　　　　　　　　　　　(*Jew of Malta*, I.)

Barabus and Ithamore.

Bara. As for myself, I walk abroad o' nights
　　　　And kill sick people, groaning under walls ;
　　　　Sometimes I go about and poison wells,
　　　　But tell me now how thou hast spent thy time.

Ithamore.   Faith, master,
          In setting Christian villages a-fire,
          Chaining of eunuchs, unbinding galley slaves.
          *   *   *   *   *
Bara.   Why this is something.   Make account of me
          As of thy fellow.   We are villains both.
                                        (*Jew of Malta*, II.)
                    Edward II.

King. What ! was I born to fly—to run away
          And leave the Mortimers conquerors behind ?
          Give me my horse.

Now, first, we assign to Marlowe the play of
'Henry VI.' or rather the second and third parts,
written probably with the assistance of Greene,
Peele, and Nash.   We believe such authorship was generally known, when Meres wrote
his 'Palladis Tamia;' and that therefore he
omitted it from the list of Shakespeare's plays.
It displays all his characteristics both of style
and sentiment; while we fancy we can see, in
the Duke of Gloster's speech, beginning " Brave
peers of England, pillars of the state " (2 Hen.
VI. I. 1), an improved reproduction of his apostrophe to Persia in Tamburlaine, already quoted.

From Meres' list we select ' Richard III.,' which
has all his characteristics, even to his own
recklessness.   It is violent from beginning to

end. The hero, confessing himself a villain at
the outset, resolves to wade through slaughter
to a throne. And in his impetuous wilfulness
not only is good taste cast aside, · probability
and even possibility are disregarded. Thus, his
courtship of the Lady Anne, ignores every
sentiment of humanity. And, if it be not a libel
on womanhood, his women possess no humanity
beyond its form. Of course the reader has
already perceived that Richard's outburst of—

> Slave, I have set my mind upon a cast,
> And I will stand the hazard of the die :
> A horse ! a horse ! my kingdom for a horse ! (V. 4.)

has been anticipated in 'Edward II.'

Peele's more important publications are the
'Arraignment of Paris,' a pastoral drama ;
'Edward I.' 'David and Bathsheba,' a tragi-
comedy ; 'Absolom' a tragedy ; 'The Tale of
Troy,' from which there is a quotation in 'Ham-
let,' (II. 2), and the 'Battle of Alcazar.' He also
published 'Discensus Astreæ ;' 'Polyhymnia ;'
'Honour of the Garter ;' 'Merry-conceited
Jests ;' and 'Anglorum Firiæ.'

Collier's judgment is that though his genius
was not boldly original, he had an elegance of

fancy, gracefulness of expression and melody of versification which, in the earlier part of his life, was scarcely approached by any contemporary; and that his 'David and Bathsheba' and 'Absolom' were the first successful essays in real pathos.

The speech from the 'Tale of Troy' given by the player in 'Hamlet,' and the following extracts, will afford fair specimens of his poetry.

Song.—Paris and Œnone.

Œn. Fair, fair and twice as fair,
  As fair as any may be
The fairest shepherd on our green
A love for any lady.
Par. Fair, fair and twice as fair
  As fair as any may be.
Thy love is fair for thee alone
And for no other lady.
Œn. My love is fair, my love is gay
  And fresh as bin the flowers in May,
And of my love the roundelay
  Concludes with Cupid's curse.
They that do change old love for new,
  Pray, gods, they change for worse.
  (Arraignment of Paris.)

Now comes my lover, tripping like a roe,
And brings my longings tangled in her hair.
T' enjoy her love I'll build a kindly bower,
Seated in hearing of a hundred streams.
  (David and Bathsheba.)

Having regard to his style, we assign the authorship of 'A Midsummer Night's Dream' to him; and we think he may also have written the 'Merchant of Venice,' the 'Two Gentlemen of Verona,' and 'King John.'

Nash is best known as a pamphleteer of keen observation and great satiric power; but he was also a poet and dramatist. He wrote, in addition to the Martin Marprelate pamphlets, 'Summer's Last Will,' a comedy, and the 'Isle of Dogs,' a satiric drama, both of which were performed before the Queen. The latter, for which he was imprisoned (Palladis Tamia), was never printed. He was collaborateur with Marlowe in the tragedy of 'Dido.' His other works were 'Pierce Penniless,' printed in 1592, 'Christ's Tears over Jerusalem' and 'Lenten Stuff,' a description of the herring-trade, both printed in 1593; and the 'Terrors of the Night,' printed in 1594.

As a poet he is inferior to Greene, Marlowe or Peele, but as a prose-writer stands first among all his contemporaries. Thus, when his orthography is modernized, his composition, as D'Israeli says, is as flowing as Addison's, with scarcely a vestige of antiquity. He abjures

both the ornaments of euphuism and the conceits
which were then so common, but is natural and
perspicacious. This must have been observed
in reading our quotations from 'Pierce Penniless' (chap. 1) and the preface to 'Menaphon'
(chap. 12). And the following will sufficiently
illustrate his blank verse :

> I never loved ambitiously to climb,
> Or thrust my hand too far into the fire,
> To be in heaven sure's a blessed thing ;
> But Atlas-like to prop heaven on our back
> Cannot but be more labour than delight.
> Such is the state of man in honour placed.
> They are gold vessels made for servile uses,
> High trees that keep the weather from low houses,
> But cannot shield the tempest from themselves.
> I love to dwell between the hills and dales,
> Neither to be so great as to be envied,
> Nor yet so poor the world should pity me.
>
> *(Summer's Last Will.)*

> Now Dido with these relics burn thyself,
> And make Æneas famous through the world
> For perjury and slaughter of a queen.
> Here lies the sword, that, in the darksome case,
> He drew and swore by, to be true to me.
> Thou shalt burn first ; thy crime is worse than his.
> Here lies the garment that I clothed him in
> When first he came on shore. Perish thou, too ;
> These letters, lines and perjured papers, all
> Shall burn to cinders in this precious flame.

And now, ye gods, that guide the starry frame
And order all things at your high dispose,
Grant through the traitor's land in Italy
They may still be tormented with unrest,
And from mine ashes let a conqueror rise
That may revenge this treason to a king. (*Dido*, V.)

The only play, mentioned by Meres, we assign to him is 'Henry IV.,' a piece in every way worthy of his scholarship and satiric observation, and whose declamation, in many parts, is level with his blank verse. We also think that he, in conjunction with Greene, was the author of 'A Winter's Tale;' and that it is the comedy to which Greene refers, as having been their joint production (see letter in the 'Groatsworth of Wit,' chapter 14). Both were well acquainted with the rogues who preyed on simple folks and could, therefore, adapt the Autolycus of Terence to the circumstances of English bumpkins, as is so cleverly done in the 'Winter's Tale.'

The reader must understand that the plays, as they now exist, are, for the most part, in a very different condition to that, in which they left the hands of their original authors; and it seems probable that, before Greene wrote his 'Groatsworth of Wit,' the work of their revision had

commenced — a work which he evidently
attributes to Shakespeare himself; such, in our
opinion, being the only meaning that can be
given to his remark, that 'the upstart crow
thought himself as well able to bombast out a
blank verse as the best of them.' Hence, we
may infer, that previous to 1592, people had
begun to talk of Shakespeare's plays, the outside
world accepting him as the author; while those
better informed regarded him only as a broker,
who had, as Ben Jonson says, bought the
reversion of old plays and, by a pretended
revision, had made each man's wit his own.
And the fact, that the revision at which both
Greene and Jonson sneer was entitled to
respect, in no way militates against our argument; because we are all inclined to despise
emendations which correct our judgment and
thereby diminish our importance.

CHAPTER XVI.

AUTHORSHIP OF THE PLAYS, CONTINUED.

The " two more " suggested by Greene—Samuel Daniel,
' Romeo and Juliet'—Thomas Lodge, ' Love's Labour
Won' ('As You Like It ').

In addition to three whom Greene specially addresses, in his ' Groatsworth of Wit,' he says
that he might add " two more," who had already
written against those " buckram gentlemen "
(the players). Both of them, we may therefore
fairly presume, had severed their connection with
Shakespeare, each having received some kind of
provocation. They were also known, at least by
reputation, to himself and the three he par-
ticularizes ; so that our enquiry, in seeking to
discover who they were, may be limited to the
poor scholars, who had resorted to the theatre
for literary employment. But we are not left to
speculate on the writings of that large class to
find some which show an affinity with the

Shakespearian drama. Direct evidence, as regards one, is immediately forthcoming.

Thus we find that during the Christmas holiday of 1598, and 1599, two plays were performed at St. John's College, Cambridge, viz. (1) 'The Pilgrimage to Parnassus;' and (2) 'The Return from Parnassus.' 'The Return from Parnassus,' performed at the same place in 1601, is a different piece, with which we have nothing now to do. It has long been known; but the other two are recent discoveries, having been found by Mr. Macrae so late as 1887, among Hearne's Collection in the Bodleian library. The authors are unknown; but, as St. John's was the College both of Greene and Nash, they were, probably, students well acquainted with their history.

No. 1, in metaphorical terms, describes college life. Two youths, Studioso and Philomusus, are represented as setting out in search of learning. They are tempted to turn aside by Madido, a drunkard; Stupido, a Puritan; Amoretto, a voluptuary; and Ingenioso, a disappointed author. They, however, persevere, and in four years reach the summit of the hill (take their A.B.).

No. 2 exhibits their struggles to get a living
after leaving the university, the result being
that Philomusus becomes a sexton, burying his
hopes along with the dead bodies of the parish;
while Studioso engages himself as a private
tutor in a family, where he is required to eat
with the servants and work in the fields during
harvest. Ingenioso, the author, is represented
as reduced to dependence on one Gallio, who
employs him to write books, which he passes off
as his own. And it is in the mouth of Ingenioso
we find the testimony to which we refer.
Gallio having given a certain passage as his own,
Ingenioso exclaims :

> Mark ! Romeo and Juliet ! O monstrous theft ! I think
> he will run through a whole book of Samuel Daniel.

Now if the words mean anything, they mean
that Samuel Daniel was known as the author of
' Romeo and Juliet.' It is saying, in fact, what
a believer in Shakespeare might say, if any one
should now give something from that tragedy as
his own composition : " Why that's from ' Romeo
and Juliet.' He'll give us a whole play of
Shakespeare's next."

And this direct evidence is confirmed by the

similarity of style, observable in Daniel's
acknowledged works and the general texture of
' Romeo and Juliet.' We limit our remark to the
general texture ; because there are many
passages in it which are wholly foreign to the
genius of Daniel, and which must be ascribed to
a reviser. But the following, pointed out by
Malone, Steevens, and, more recently, by Daniel,
in his preface to 'The Tragical History,' are
really parallels from ' Romeo and Juliet' (V. 3).

> Oh ! my love ! my wife !
> Death that hath suck'd the honey of thy breath
> Hath had no power yet upon thy beauty,
> Thou art not conquer'd : *beauty's ensign yet*
> *Is crimson in thy lips* and in thy cheeks,
> And death's pale flag is not advanced there.
> * * * * * Ah ! dear Juliet,
> Why art thou yet so fair ? Shall I believe
> That unsubstantial death is amorous,
> And that the lean abhorred monster keeps
> Thee here, in dark, to be his paramour ?
> * * * * * Eyes, look your last !
> Arms, take your last embrace ; and lips, oh ! you
> The doors of breath, seal with a righteous kiss.

And from Daniel's ' Complaint of Rosamond :'

> Ah ! how methinks I see Death dallying seeks,
> To entertain himself in Love's sweet place !

Decayéd roses of discoloured cheeks
Do yet retain dear notes of former grace,
And ugly Death sits fair within her face.

* * * * *

And nought-respecting Death, the last of pains,
Placed his *pale colours, th' ensign* of his might,
  Upon his new-got spoil . . . . . .
Pitiful mouth, said he, that living gavest
  The sweetest comfort that my soul could wish,
Oh ! be it lawful now that dead thou havest
  The sorrowful farewell of a dying kiss.
  And you, fair eyes, containers of my bliss,
Motives of love born to be matchéd never,
Entombed in your sweet circles, sleep for ever.

We have nothing under Daniel's hand attacking the players; but, if we give effect to the opposition raised to the publication of the fourth 4to edition of 'Romeo and Juliet,' we may assume that he did write something against those "buckram gentlemen."

As regards the second of the "two more" we have only circumstantial evidence; but it seems to point very distinctly to THOMAS LODGE. He had been a dramatist and the collaborateur of Greene; and in 1589 he had emphatically renounced plays and players, as we showed in a quotation from 'Glaucus and Scylla,' in our first chapter; while '*As You Like It*' '(Love's Labour's

P

Won)' is undoubtedly a dramatization of his
novel of ' *Rosalind*.' It is not only the same
plot or story, the following extract from a song
in 'Rosalind' gives us the type of the love-sick
swain, who hangs verses on the trees, in the
play :

> Turn I my looks unto the skies
> Love, with his arrows, wounds my eyes ;
> If so I gaze upon the ground,
> Love then in every flower is found ;
> Search I the shades to fly my pain,
> Love meets me in the shade again. (*Rosalind.*)

In comparing ' *Rosalind* ' with ' *As You Like
It*,' we compare a very silly novel and a very
clever play ; but the difference is due to the
reviser, who has rewritten rather than revised ;
so that the comedy published for the first time
in the folio of 1623 was practically another work
than that mentioned by Meres in 1598.

CHAPTER XVII.

AUTHORSHIP OF THE PLAYS, CONTINUED.

George Chapman—*Macbeth* and the *Tempest*.

But Greene's suggestion of authors is not yet exhausted. Beside those he addresses and the "two more" he might add, he refers to "other new-comers," whom he leaves to "the mercy of those painted monsters." No clue, however, presents itself, when we begin to enquire who those new-comers were ; and though, in looking through Stowe's list of poets who flourished during Elizabeth's reign, our eye is naturally caught by such names as George Chapman, Michael Drayton, Ben Jonson, and Thomas Dekkar,—yet we see no reason for choosing any of them. They all knew Shakespeare, more or less, when Greene died ; but so did many more who cannot be suspected of contributing to his drama. Our only guide, therefore, is similarity of style ; and that points to Chapman as the

original author of *Macbeth* and the *Tempest*.
And nothing in his character or circumstances is
inconsistent with such a conclusion. He was, to
be sure, a person of respectable habits, and all
his known plays were produced by Henslowe
and Alleyne; but he was a poor man and a
successful dramatist, and they were facts a
keen man of business, like Shakespeare, was not
likely to overlook. The first we have already
noticed (Chap. I.), and the second is no less
certain. *The Blind Beggar of Alexandria*
and *Bussie d'Ambois* had been immensely
popular. Indeed, Nathaniel Field was as celebrated in the latter, as Richard Burbage was in
Richard III. We do not, of course, suggest
that ' Macbeth ' and the ' Tempest ' must already
have been written when Greene died (1592).
Nor is it necessary we should, since Greene's
words imply, that he was looking forward, when
he spoke of the " other new-comers." But their
not having been printed until they made their
appearance in the Folio of 1623 proves nothing;
because neither the ' Comedy of Errors,' nor the
' Two Gentlemen of Verona,' were printed any
sooner, though Meres refers to them both in
1598.

But 'Macbeth' and the 'Tempest' are not only in his style, they remind us of his special qualification. He was one of the great classical scholars of his age, and both of them are founded on classical models. His published works, in fact, give an air of consistency to our pretence. He wrote eighteen plays, of which the *Blind Beggar of Alexandria, Bussie d'Ambois, Byron's Conspiracy, All Fools, Gentleman Usher*, and the *Widow's Tears* are best known, the last being remembered on account, of the grotesque incident which made the widow, in the midst of her lamentations for the deceased, fall in love with the sentinel who was guarding his corpse. But his great works were his translations of the *Iliad, Odyssey, Epigrams and Batrachomyomachia** of Homer, the *Shield of Hercules* and the *Works and Days* of Hesiod, and Juvenal's fifth *Satire*. He also completed Marlowe's fragment of *Hero and Leander*.

His diction, always rugged, is often barbarous, while false elevation and extravagant metaphor spoil his most forcible passages. He is said to

---

* The hymns of Homer were unknown in Chapman's time. They were discovered at Moscow in the eighteenth century and edited by Ruhnken.

have been the first who introduced into English
the compound epithets of the Greek. The
following extracts will we think, confirm our
description of his style :

Terror of darkness, O thou king of flames,
That, with thy *music-footed* horse, doth strike
The clear light out of crystal or dark earth,
And hurl'st the instinctive fire about the world,
Wake, wake the ·drowsy and enchanted night,
That sleeps with dead eyes in this heavy riddle.
Or, thou, great prince of shades, where never sun
Sticks his *far-darted* beams, whose eyes are made
To see in darkness and see ever best,
Where sense is blindest, open now the heart
Of thy abashed oracle, that, for fear
Of some ill it includes, would fain lie hid,
And rise thou with it in thy greater light.

(Bussie d'Ambois.)

I tell thee love is nature's second sun,
Causing a spring of virtues where he shines ;
And as without the sun, the world's great age,
All colours, beauties both of art and nature
Are given in vain to men—so, without love,
All beauties, bred in women, are in vain.

(All Fools.)

No longer could the day nor destinies
Delay the night, who now did frowning rise
Into his throne ; and at her humourous breasts
Visions and dreams lay sucking.   All men's rest

Fall, like the mists of death, upon their eyes ;
Day's *too-long* darts so killed their faculties.

                (*Hero and Leander*, 6th Ses.)

Now *Macbeth* discloses all the peculiarities we have mentioned. Thus, we have in it no less than twenty-one compound epithets, only five of which were sufficiently appropriate to retain a place in our language; viz., *rump-fed* and *tempest-tost* (I. 3) ; *temple-haunting* (I. 6) ; *even-handed* and *trumpet-tongued* (I. 7) ; *nose-painting* (II. 3) ; *dismal-fatal* (III. 6) ; *ditch-delivered, birth-strangled, lion-mottled, earth-bound, waspish-headed* and *high-placed* (IV. 1) ; *gold-bound* and *blood-boltered* (IV. 2) ; *shag-eared, summer-seeding, bloody-sceptred* and *strangely-visited* (IV. 3) ; *cream-faced* and *thick-coming* (V. 3). This *bombast* faces us everywhere. Thus :

                The merciless Macdonald
Worthy to be a rebel—for to that
The multiplying *villanies* of nature
Do *swarm* upon him—from the western isle
Of Kernes and Gallowglasses is supplied,
And fortune, on his damned quarrel smiling,
Shewed like a rebel's whore.   But all's too weak,
For brave Macbeth—well he deserves the name—
Disdaining fortune, with his brandished steel,
Carved out his passage, till he faced the slave.   (I. 2.)

To *uncouthness*, unsurpassed and unsurpassable in—

> All our service
> In every point twice done and then done double
> Were poor and single business to contend
> Against those honours deep and broad wherewith
> Your Majesty loads our house.　　　　(I. 6.)

And so *extravagant metaphor* in

> His virtues,
> Will plead like angels trumpet-tongued, against .
> The deep damnation of his taking off;
> And pity, like *a naked new-born babe*,
> *Striding the blast*, or heaven's cherubim horsed
> Upon the sightless couriers of the air,
> Shall blow the horrid deed in every eye,
> That *tears shall drown the wind.*　　　(I. 7.)

No doubt there are passages in 'Macbeth' superior to anything Chapman ever wrote or could have written; but they only show the tragedy was revised after it left his hands.

The *Tempest*, too, in its general style has all Chapman's peculiarities. It has such compound epithets as *wide-chapped* (I. 1); *under-going, sight-outrunning, up-staring,* and *hag-born* (I. 2); *be-mocked-at* (III. 3); *sour-eyed, white-cold, lass-lorn, rocky-hard, short-grassed,* and *dove-drawn*

(IV. 1); and *green-sour* (V. 1). It does not afford metaphors so extravagant as 'Macbeth'; but that was not to be expected in a comedy. The following passages, however, are sufficiently bombastic and uncouth.

> Ye elves of hills, brooks, standing lakes and groves,
> And ye, that on the sands with printless foot
> Do chase the ebbing Neptune and do fly him,
> When he comes back ; you demy-puppets that
> By moonshine do the green-sour ringlets make,
> Whereof the ewe not bites, and you, whose pastime
> Is to make midnight mushrooms, that rejoice
> To hear the solemn curfew, by whose aid—
> Weak masters though ye be—I have bedimmed
> The noontide sun, called forth the mutinous winds,
> And twixt the green sea and the azured vault
> Set roaring war.   (V. 1.)

> I have done nothing but in care of thee,
> Of thee, my dear one, thee, my daughter, who
> Art ignorant of what thou art, nought knowing
> Of whence I am, nor that I am *more better**
> Than Prospero, master of a full, poor cell
> And thy no greater father.   (I. 2.)

The 'Tempest' has never been assigned to any one but Shakespeare; but it has been suggested that Middleton may have been the

---

* This comparing of a comparative was unusual in English even then. Chapman, however, would adopt it as being *more Græco.*

original author of 'Macbeth.' The suggestion,
however, only rests on the fact that he wrote a
play called 'The Witch.' But a belief in witches
was general in those days ; so that any author
might have made use of them.

CHAPTER XVIII.

AUTHORSHIP OF THE PLAYS, CONTINUED.

Francis Bacon, author of ' Hamlet.'

WE have left our greatest author till last; but his claim is not heard of for the first time to-day. This idea, as far as we know, was originally started by Horace Walpole, he, and those who followed him, maintaining that Bacon wrote all Shakespeare's plays. He concluded—and the conclusion was not unworthy of his natural sagacity—that works of such pre-eminent merit, could only be ascribed to the known genius of " the wisest and brightest of mankind," and not to a person of whose genius there was no independent evidence. It was, in his case, a *primâ facie* conclusion, for, in his time, historical research had not been brought to bear on the subject. But in 1856 such research began, a work being then published under the title of, ' Was Lord Bacon the author of Shakespeare's Plays?' in a letter to Lord Ellesmere, by W. H. Smith, London, 1856, 8vo. Miss Delia Bacon followed the next year with ' The Philosophy of Shakespeare's Plays unfolded,' London, 1857. Seven years after that came ' The Authorship of Shakespeare,' by N. Holmes, a judge of the Supreme Court of Missouri, New York, 1866, in 8vo ; and finally ' The Great Cryptogram,' London, 1888. All of these, with the exception of the last, are, we think, entitled to respectful consideration. But we are not now proposing to deal with that large question, but with the smaller issue raised by Nash's preface to ' Menaphon, viz., the authorship of ' Hamlet.'

His testimony in that is that the author of ' Hamlet ' was not only a lawyer himself, but the son of a lawyer—one born in the trade of *Noverint*. And we take Lord Campbell's opinion as conclusive that he was a lawyer of no common type, that he was one who had greater legal knowledge than " many a practising barrister." Now Nash, it must be born in mind, was a contemporary both of Bacon and Shakespeare, and evidently knew what he was talking about. We attach no importance to the sneering suggestion of the author's want of latinity. It is obviously a piece of gratuitous impertinence, due only to envy. And we can easily believe that Nash !was envious, because the appearance of ' Hamlet' must have thrown into the shade all the dramas with which he and his friends had previously supplied the stage. In other respects his testimony bears truth on its face, when we apply it to Bacon. He was a lawyer who had " run through every art and thriven by none." He had not only projected a new philosophy, he had been a diplomatist in France, and a courtier, barrister, and member of Parliament at home; and he certainly had not yet thriven by any of those employments. We, therefore, conclude that Nash and everybody in the literary and theatrical world knew that the young barrister and member for Taunton was the author of the tragedy which was so unlike those that had preceded it.

And nothing in Bacon's character, or genius contradicts that conclusion. Even his personal appearance in youth suggested the dramatist. Thus Hepworth Dixon, says :

How he appears in outward grace and aspect, the miniature of Hilyard helps us to conceive. Slight in build, rosy and round in flesh, the head well-set and erect, a bloom of study and travel in the fat, girlish face, which looks even younger than his years; the hat and feather tossed aside from the broad, white brow, over which crisps and curls a mane of dark, soft hair; an English nose, firm, open, straight, a mouth delicate and small—*a lady or a jester's mouth, a thousand pranks and humours, quibbles, whims and laughters lurking in its twinkling, tremulous lines.* Such is Francis Bacon at the age of twenty-four (1585). (*Personal Hist. of Lord Bacon*, p. 22.)

And a graver biographer goes farther towards giving us a character fit for the author of that famous tragedy :

Those talents, Mallet remarks, that commonly appear single in others, shone forth in him united. All his contemporaries, even those who hated the courtier, stand up and bear witness to the superior abilities of the writer and pleader, of the philosopher and companion. In conversation *he could assume the most different characters and speak the language proper to each, with a facility that was perfectly natural,* or the dexterity of the habit concealed every appearance of art.

(*Mallet's Works*, III. 223.)

Then Ben Jonson's description of his speaking suggests one, who could have written speeches which would have been quite as effective, when put into the mouth of an actor. Thus he calls him—

A noble speaker who was full of gravity in his speaking. His language, *where he could spare and pass by a jest*, was nobly censorious. No man ever spoke more neatly, more pressly, more weightily, or suffered less idleness, less emptiness in what he uttered. No member of his speech but consisted of his own graces. His hearers could not cough, or look aside from him without loss. He commanded where he spoke and had his judges angry and pleased at his devotion. No man had their affections more in his power. The fear of every man that heard him was lest he should make an end. (*Jonson's Works*, III. p. 401.)

Let us confirm this by an extract from the speeches delivered at a Conference of Pleasure, devised by Lord Essex, where various persons were called on to exercise their wit.

My praise, he said, shall be dedicated to the mind itself. The mind is the man, and the knowledge of the mind. A man is but what he knoweth. The mind itself is but an accident to knowledge ; for knowledge is a double of that which is. The truth of being and the truth of knowing is all one. . . .

And is not the pleasure of the intellect greater than the pleasure of the affections? Is it not a true and only pleasure of which there is no satiety? Is it not knowledge that doth alone clear the mind of all perturbations? How many things we esteem and value otherwise than they are? This ill-proportioned estimation, these vain imaginations—these be the clouds of error that turn into the storms of perturbation. . . .

Is this but a vein of delight and not of discovery, of

contentment and not of benefit? Shall we not as well discern the riches of nature's warehouse as the benefit of her shop? Is truth ever barren? Shall we not be able thereby to produce worthy effects and to endow the life of man with infinite commodities.

But shall I make this garland to be put on a wrong head? Would anyone believe me, if I should verify this upon the knowledge that is now in use? Are we the richer by one poor invention, by reason of all the learning that hath been these many hundred years? The industry of artificers maketh some small improvement of things invented; and chance sometimes, in experimenting, maketh us to stumble upon somewhat which is new; but all the disputations of the learned never brought to light one effect of nature before unknown. . . . .

Therefore, no doubt the sovereignty of man lieth hid in knowledge, wherein many things are reserved, which kings with their treasure cannot buy, nor with their forces command. Their spy-alls and intelligencers can give no news of them; their seamen and discoverers cannot sail where they grow. Now we govern nature in opinions; but we are thrall unto her in necessity. But, if we would be led by her in invention, we should command her in action.

(Bacon's Works, II. 123.)

Now this, we boldly assert, is the style of 'Hamlet,' a style, where every phrase might be the text of a separate discourse.

But why, it may be asked, was not 'Hamlet' included in Bacon's works if he were known as the author? Why, we may ask in return, was *no poetry* included in them, except two or three psalms? We have it on the evidence of Stow, that he was known as a poet. His words, which admit of no other interpretation, are :

> Our modern and excellent poets, *which worthily flourish in their works*—and all of them in my own knowledge lived together in this queen's reign—according to their priorities, as near as I could, I have orderly set down.
>
> Geo. Gascoyne, Esq., Tho. Churchward, Esq., Sir Edward Dyer, Knt., Edmond Spenser, Esq., Sir Philip Sidney, Knt., Sir John Harrington, Knt., Sir Tho. Challoner, Knt., *Sir Francis Bacon, Knt.*, Sir John Davie, Knt., Master John Lily, Gent., M. Geo. Chapman, M. Wm. Warner, Gent., M. William Shakspeare, Gent., Samuel Daniel, Esq., Michael Draiton, Esq. of the Bath, Master Christopher Marlo, Gent., M. Benjamin Johnson, Gent., John Marston, Esq., M. Abraham Francis, Gent., Master Francis Meres, Gent., Master Josua Silvester, Gent., Master Tho. Dekkar, Gent., M. John Fletcher, Gent., M. Jno. Webster, Gent., M. Tho. Heywood, Gent., M. Tho. Middleton, Gent., M. Geo. Wither.
>
> (*Annals or General Chronicle of England.*)

Here he figures along with such well-known poets as Spenser, Lily, Chapman, Daniel, Drayton, Marlowe, and Ben Jonson, as well as Shakspeare himself; so that there can be no doubt he was as much an acknowledged poet as any of them. But we can easily understand, that he, himself, regarded his poetry as a

Q

juvenile performance unworthy to appear among
his greater and graver works—works of whose
importance he was fully conscious. And,
considering that Nash speaks of 'Hamlet' as
having been already written in 1589, it must
have been composed before Bacon had reached
his twenty-eighth year. When, however, we
begin to examine the piece we recognize his
genius and peculiarities at every step. And
they are the more remarkable, because they are
so different to those of contemporary authors.
While they love to appeal to classic mythology
and overlook all but nature's more striking
phenomena, he ignores the fables of antiquity
and fixes his mind on nature in all even its
minutest forms, and thence finds illustration for
his most serious teaching. Thus we read :

1. The canker galls the infants of the Spring
   Too oft before their buttons be disclos'd ;
   And in the morn and liquid dew of youth
   Contagious blastments are most imminent. (I. 3.)

2. The glow-worm shows the matin to be near
   And 'gins to pale his ineffectual fire. (*Id.*)

3. Your bedded hair, like life in excrements,
   Starts up and stands on end. (III. 4.)

4. This (war for a trifle) is the imposthume of much wealth
   and peace,

That inward breaks and shows no cause without
Why the man dies. (IV. 4.)

5. There lives, within the very flame of love,
A kind of wick or snuff, that will abate it;
And nothing is at a like goodness still;
For goodness, growing to a pleurisy,
Dies in his own too much. (IV. 7.)

Then many of the more striking sentiments expressed in the play are to be found in Bacon's essays. Thus:

1.   The dram of *base*
Doth all the noble substance often dout
To his own scandal. (I. 4.)

And in Essay No. 1 :

A mixture of falsehood in dealing is like *alloy* in coin of gold and silver, which may make the metal work the better, but it embaseth it.

2. Let him go, Gertrude, do not fear our person.
There's such *divinity* doth hedge a king
That treason can but peep to what it would. (IV. 5.)

And in Essay 58 :

A King is a mortal *god* on earth.

3. Too much of water hast thou, poor Ophelia;
And therefore, I forbid my tears. But yet
It is our trick; nature her custom holds
Let shame say what it will. (IV. 7.)

And in Essay 38 :

Nature is often hidden, sometimes overcome, seldom extinguished.

4.   To die, to sleep !
   To sleep, perchance to dream ! Ay, there's the rub ;
   For, in that sleep of death, what dreams may come
   When we have shuffled off this mortal coil,
   Must give us pause.   There's the respect
   That makes calamity of so long life.
   For who would bear the whips and scorns of time,
   The oppressor's wrong, the proud man's contumely,
      *   *   *   *   *   *
   That patient merit of the unworthy takes
   When he himself might his quietus make
   With a bare bodkin ? who would fardels bear
   To grunt and sweat under a weary life,
   But that the dread of something after death.
   The undiscover'd country, from whose bourn
   No traveller returns—puzzles the will,
   And makes us rather bear those ills we have
   Than fly to others that we know not of ?   (III. 1.)

And in Essay 2 :

Men fear death as children fear to go in the dark.

And while we are observing these coincidences, the legal knowledge displayed by the dramatist must come as strong confirmation of Bacon's authorship, there having been no other lawyer, at that day, equal to its composition.   And we say this without forgetting that the authors of 'Gorboduc' and 'Cambyses' both were LL.D.

Nor must we neglect to notice the "idle conceits and contemptible equivocations" of which Dr. Johnson complains; for they were faults to which Bacon was always prone. That they often spoilt his rare eloquence when speaking cannot be doubted; because Ben Jonson, when describing it, expressly limits his praise to those occasions, when he could "spare and pass by a jest."

We do not, however, hold Bacon responsible for the fustian, which takes the form of awkward and absurd amplifications of that we have already given an example (Chapter III.), and we will now add two more, placing the amplification in Italics.

The queen, who is remarking to 'Hamlet' on his grief, asks why his father's death seems so particular. On which he says :

Seems, madam! nay it is. I know not seems.
'Tis not alone my inky cloak, good mother,
Nor customary suits of solemn black,
Nor windy suspirations of forc'd breath,
No, nor the fruitful river in the eye,

Nor the dejected haviour of the visage,
Together with all forms, modes, shows of grief
That can denote me truly.   These, indeed, "seem ; "
For they are actions that a man might play ;
But I have that within that passeth show ;
These but the trappings and the suits of woe.   (I. 2.)

The second is in Ophelia's beautiful speech :

Oh ! what a noble mind is here o'erthrown !
The courtier's, soldier's, scholar's eye, tongue, sword ;
The expectancy and rose of the fair state,
The glass of fashion and the mould of form.   (III. 1.)

Now the reader cannot fail to observe how complete and harmonious the passages are without the amplification—how confused and unsatisfactory with it.   Shall we commit the absurdity of thinking, that our author, who could write such beautiful passages, would choose so to entangle them ?   Must we not rather conclude that the amplifications were the work of an incompetent reviser ?   Henslowe's Diary contains several entries of payments to authors for improving other people's plays ; and Shakespeare a shrewd, but illiterate man of business, might very naturally have employed some experienced dramatist to revise this first attempt of the young lawyer? And an experienced dramatist might easily have amended its very defective dramatic construction. Instead of that, he seems to have seized. on some of the finest speeches and tried to amend what was beyond amendment.

CHAPTER XIX.

AUTHORSHIP OF THE PLAYS, CONTINUED.

Francis Bacon, the Reviser.

It is quite likely that Shakespeare, after the success of 'Hamlet'—and of its success there can be no doubt—should propose to Bacon the revision of all the plays he obtained from other authors ; and that Bacon's want of money, which Hepworth Dixon has so vividly portrayed, may have induced Bacon to accept this proposal. And that, in our opinion, is what actually occurred. But we can all understand that Bacon would wish the fact kept secret. To have written a play was one thing—the Earl of Dorset and the Master of Trinity Hall, Cambridge, had done the same—but it was another thing to figure as the paid servant of the players, men whose evil life and pernicious example were a constant theme of animadversion to the municipal authorities of London and West-

minster. No doubt the Court patronized them ;
but it was only as it patronized the bulls, bears,
and apes, which were baited for the queen's
amusement. Shakespeare would, of course, be
willing to keep the secret, being far too keen to
overlook the advantage of posing as author of
the dramas he was producing. We think, it
was this revision which Greene mistook for
Shakespeare's own work, when he said, he
supposes he is " as well able to bombast out a
blank verse, as the best of you ; and, being an
absolute *Johannes Factotum*, is, in his own
conceit, the only Shake-scene in a country."

And such revision is all that the more
reasonable commentators claim for William
Shakespeare. Thus Malone, writing in 1790,
says of the second and third parts of 'Henry
VI.' :

The *Contention of the two famous houses of York and
Lancaster*, in two parts, was published in 4to in 1600 ; and
the first part was entered on the stationer's, as Mr. Steevens
has observed, March 12th 1593–4. On these two plays,
which I believe to have been written by some preceding
author before 1590, Shakespeare formed, as I conceive, this
and the following drama, altering, retrenching or amplifying
as he thought proper. . . .

All the lines printed in the usual manner (in Malone's
edition) are found in the original 4to plays, or, at least

with such minute variations as are not worth mentioning; and those, I conceive, Shakespeare adopted as he found them.   The lines to which inverted commas are prefixed, were, if my hypothesis be well founded, retouched and greatly improved by him; and those with asterisks were his own original production.—the embroidery with which he ornamented the coarse stuff, that had been awkwardly made up for the stage, by some of his contemporaries.

(Malone's Shakespeare, London, 1790, Preface to 2 Henry VI.)

Now if we adapt Malone's plan of distinction we shall, as a rule, have common-place and absurd declamation as the original composition, and adopt the fine passages as the work of the reviser.   We say as a rule, because it appears to us, that in 'Romeo and Juliet,' and 'Othello' the revision, that is apparent, is not a literary improvement, the general character of the composition being excellent.   But in the majority of cases the revision constitutes the beauty.   This is especially remarkable in *Macbeth*, where such passages, as the following, are in striking contrast with the general uncouthness and bombast :—

> The sleeping and the dead
> Are but as pictures; 'tis the eye of childhood
> That fears a painted devil.   (II. 3.)

I have liv'd long enough : my way of life
Is fall'n into the sear and yellow leaf ;
And that which should accompany old age,
As honour, love, obedience, troops of friends,
I must not look to have. (V. 3.)

To-morrow, and to-morrow, and to-morrow
Creeps in this petty pace from day to`day,
To the last syllable of recorded time ;
And all our yesterdays have lighted fools
The way to dusty death. Out, out, brief candle !
Life's but a walking shadow ; a poor player,
That struts and frets his hour upon the stage,
And then is heard no more. (V. 5.)

Or this, in *Twelfth Night* :—

> She never told her love,
> But let concealment, like a worm i' the bud,
> Feed on her damask cheek. (II. 4.)

Or this, in *Measure for Measure* :—

> Great men may jest with saints. 'Tis wit in them ;
> But, in the less, foul profanation.

But if those indicate the work of revision, the
parallels in Bacon's work point out the reviser.
And the first thing that strikes us is, that
Bacon's tone of thought is the tone of thought
in the plays. There may be—there necessarily

would be, some concession to popular prejudice; but we occasionally meet with almost startling protests against it.   And in that day he was almost, if not quite alone, in protesting against such prejudices.   Thus hostility to the Jews was common to Englishmen, and the 'Merchant of Venice,' as we formerly showed, was, in its general scope, a pandering to that unworthy sentiment.   Yet who could, or can, gainsay the words put into the mouth of Shylock?

> He hath disgraced me and hindered me of half-a-million, laughed at my losses, mocked at my gains, scorned my nation, thwarted my bargains, cooled my friends, heated my enemies; and what's his reason?   *I am a Jew.*   Hath not a Jew eyes?   Hath not a Jew hands, organs, dimensions, senses, affections, passions? fed with the same food . . . . as a Christian is? if you prick us, do we not bleed? if you tickle us, do we not laugh? if you poison us do we not die? and if you wrong us, shall we not revenge?   (III. 1.)

Who, in the sixteenth century would have written so but Francis Bacon?

Then we have parallels in sentiment which, allowing for the differences of prose and verse, and of serious and comic humour, present themselves in the same form.   They are so numerous that we can only take one here and there; but a few will be sufficient to demonstrate our proposition.

Beginning with his ' Essays,' we read :—

What is truth ? said jesting Pilate and would not wait for an answer; and certainly there be that delight in giddiness and count it a bondage to *fix a belief.* (No. 1.)

And in *Much Ado about Nothing* Beatrice says of Benedick :—

He hath every month a new sworn brother. . . . He wears *his faith but as the fashion of his hat,* it ever changes with the next block. (I. 1.)

Again :—

Men fear death as children fear to go in the dark.
                                                (No. 2.)

And in *Measure for Measure* Claudio says :—

Aye ; but to die and go we know not where ;
To lie in cold obstruction and to rot ;
This sensible, warm motion to become
A kneaded clod. . . . 'tis too horrible.   (III. 1.)

Again :—

He that hath wife and children hath given hostages to fortune ; for they are impediments to great enterprises, either of virtue, or mischief. (No. 8.)

And in *All's Well that Ends Well* we have :—

A young man married, is a man that's marr'd.   (II. 3.)

And in *Much Ado about Nothing* :—

Shall I never see a bachelor of threescore again ?   Go to, i'faith, an thou wilt needs *thrust thy neck into a yoke, wear the print of it* and sigh away Sundays.   (I. 1.)

Again :—

The stage is more beholding to love than the life of man. For as to the stage, love is ever matter of comedies and now and then of tragedies.   But in life it (love) doth much mischief, sometimes like a syren, sometimes like a fury. . .
(No. 10.)

And in the *Two Gentlemen of Verona* we have :—

To be
In love, where scorn is bought with groans, coy looks,
With heart-sore sighs, one fading moment's mirth
With twenty watchful, weary, tedious nights.
If haply won, perhaps a hapless gain,
If lost, why then a grievous labour won.   (I. 1.)

And in *A Midsummer Night's Dream* :—

Things base and vile, holding no quantity
Love can transpose to form and dignity. (I. 1.)

Again, in the same Essay (No. 10) :—

You may observe that, among all the great and worthy persons, whereof the memory remaineth either ancient or recent, there is not one that hath been transported to the mad degree of love.

And in *As You Like It* Rosalind says :—

Leander would have lived many a fair year, though Hero had turned nun, if it had not been for a hot midsummer night; for, good youth, he went. but forth to wash him in the Hellespont, and being taken with the cramp, was drowned ; and the foolish chroniclers of the time found it was "Hero of Sestos." But these are all lies ; men have died from time to time, and worms have eaten them, but not for love. (IV. 1.)

Again :—

Travel in the younger sort is a part of education ; in the elder, a part of experience. . . . and let a man's travel appear rather in his discourse, than in his apparel or gesture. (No. 18.)

And in *Two Gentlemen of Verona* : —

Cease to persuade, my loving Proteus,
Home-keeping youth have ever homely wits.
     *   *   *   . *   *
I rather would entreat thy company
To see the wonders of the world abroad,
Than, living dully sluggardiz'd at home,
Wear out thy youth with shapeless idleness. (I. 1.)

And in *As You Like It* :—

Farewell, monsieur Traveller. Look you lisp and wear strange suits ; or I will scarce think you have swam in a gondola. (IV. 1.)

Again :—

It is a miserable state of mind to have few things to desire and many things to fear ; and yet that is commonly the case of kings. (No. 19.)

And in *Henry V.* we have :—

> O hard condition ! twin-born with greatness,
> Subjected to the breath of every fool !
> * * * * * *
> What kind of god art thou that suffer'st more
> Of mortal griefs, than do thy worshippers ? (IV. 1.)

And in *Richard II.* :—

> Let us sit upon the ground,
> And tell sad stories of the death of kings :
> How some have been depos'd, some slain in war ;
> Some haunted by the ghosts they have depos'd,
> Some poison'd by their wives, some sleeping kill'd,
> All murder'd. (III. 2.)

Again :—

Suspicions, amongst thoughts, are like bats amongst birds : they ever fly by twilight. (No. 31.)

And in 1 *Henry IV.* we have :—

It cannot be
The king should keep his word in loving us.
· He will suspect us still and find a time
To punish this offence in other faults.
Suspicion shall be all stuck full of eyes.

*   *   *   *   *

Look how we can, or sad or merrily,
Interpretation will misquote our looks.   (V. 2.)

Again :—

Nature is often hidden, sometimes overcome, seldom extinguished.   (No. 38.)

And in *Cymbeline* we have :—

How hard it is to hide the sparks of nature !
These boys know little, they are sons to the king,
They think they are mine; and, though trained up thus
    meanly
I' the cave, wherein they bow, their thoughts do hit
The roof of palaces.   (III. 3.)

And in *Much Ado about Nothing* :—

Wisdom and blood combating . . . . we have ten proofs to
one that blood hath the victory.   (II. 3.)

Again :—

But chiefly the mould of a man's fortune is in his own
hands. (No. 40.)

R

And in *Julius Cæsar* we read :—

> Men, at some time, are masters of their fates.
> The fault, dear Brutus, is not in our stars
> But in ourselves, that we are underlings.   (I. 2.)

And in *All's Well that Ends Well :—*

> Our remedies oft in ourselves do lie
> Which we ascribe to heaven.   (I. 1.)

Again, in the same ' Essay ' :—

> If a man look sharply and attentively, he shall *see*
> fortune ; for though she be blind, yet she is not invisible.

And in *Julius Cæsar* we have :—

> There is a tide in the affairs of men,
> Which, taken at the flood, leads on to fortune :
> Omitted, all the voyage of their life
> Is bound in shallows and in miseries.   (IV. 3.)

And in 2 *Henry IV.* :—

> There is a history in all men's lives,
> Figuring the nature of the times deceas'd,
> The which observ'd, a man may prophecy,
> With a near aim, of the main chance of things
> As yet not come to life.   (III. 1.)

Again, in his *Ornamenta Rationalia* we have :—

Oh, life! an age to him that is in misery, and to him that is happy a moment.   (No. 36.)

And in *The Merchant of Venice* Antonio says :—

> It is still her (Fortune's) use
> To let the wretched man outlive his wealth,
> To view, with hollow eye and wrinkled brow,
> An age of poverty.   .   (IV. 1.)

And in *Henry VIII.* :—

> This is the state of man.   To-day he puts forth
> The tender leaves of hope, to-morrow blossoms,
> And bears his blushing honours thick upon him.
> The third day comes a frost, a killing frost,
> And, when he thinks, good, easy man, full surely
> His greatness is a ripening, nips his root,
> And then he falls, as I do.   (III. 2.)

Again, in his *Charge against the Earl of Somerset*, we read :—

> But, my lords, it is a principle in nature, that the best things are, in their corruption, the worst, and the sweetest wine maketh the sharpest vinegar—so it fell out with them (Somerset and Sir Thomas Overbury) that this excess, if I may so term it, of friendship, ended in mortal hatred.
>
> (IV. 478)

And in *Richard II.* we have :—

> Sweet love I see, changing his property,
> Turns to the sourest and most deadly hate. (III. 2.)

R 2

And in *A Midsummer Night's Dream* :—

> For, as a surfeit of the sweetest things
> The deepest loathing to the stomach brings ;
> Or, as the heresies that men do leave,
> Are hated most of those they did deceive ;
> So thou, my surfeit and my heresy,
> Of all be hated ; but the most of me !   (II. 3.)

Again, in his *Natural History* we are told that :—

The murmur of wind in the woods, without apparent wind, shows wind to follow. (IX. 818.)

And in the First Part of *Henry IV.* we read :—

> The southern wind
> Doth play the trumpet to his purposes ;
> And, by his hollow whistling in the leaves,
> Foretells a tempest, and a blustering day. (V. 1.)

Again :—

Some putrefactions and excrements do yield excellent odours, as civet and musk. (IX. 835.)

And in *As You Like It* Touchstone remarks that :—

Civet is of a baser birth than tar ; the very uncleanly flux of a cat. (III. 2.)

Again, respecting sympathy, the history puts the following case :—

> As if two friends should agree that such a day in the week, they, being in far distant places, should pray one for another. (X. 987.)

And in *Cymbeline* Imogen complains of not having had the opportunity of making such an agreement with Leonatus :—

> Ere I could tell him
> How I would think on him at certain hours
> . . . . or have charg'd him
> At the sixth hour of morn, at noon, at midnight,
> To encounter me with orisons . . comes in my father.
> (I. 4.)

Then Bacon's special qualifications are special characteristics of the plays. He was a lawyer, and Lord Campbell has pointed out the extensive knowledge of law to be found in the plays (*Shakespeare's Legal Acquirements*). He had been a close student of Aristotle ; and Riddle has given us *Illustrations of Aristotle drawn from Shakespeare's Dramatic Works*. He was well skilled in anatomy, disease, and medicine, and no less than three competent witnesses have found evidence of such skill in the plays : viz.,

W. Wadd (*Medico-Chirurgical Commentary on Shakespeare*, 'Quarterly Journal of Science,' 1829); Dr. Stearn (*Shakespeare's Medical Knowledge*, New York, 1865); and Dr. Kellog (*Shakespeare's Delineation of Insanity, Imbecility, and Suicide*, New York, 1866).

We pass over the classical knowledge, and the knowledge of Spanish and Italian literature; because, though they formed important items in his erudition, they were common to scholars of the time, and therefore furnish no argument in support of our theory. But the illustrations, drawn from a close observance of animate and inanimate nature, are so peculiar to him that we must give some of the more striking of them.

Thus in the *Tempest* we read :—

1. Now would I give a thousand furlongs of sea for an acre of barren ground ; long heath, brown furze, anything. (I. 1.)

2. For all the rest, They'll take suggestion, as a cat laps milk. (II. 1.)

3. All the infections that the sun sucks up From bogs, fens, flats, on Prospero fall. (II. 2.)

II. From *Two Gentlemen of Verona* :—

4. As the most forward bud Is eaten by the canker ere it blow. (I. 1.)

From *Twelfth Night* :—

5.   Not yet old enough for a man, nor young enough for a boy ; as a squash is before 'tis a peascod, or a codling when 'tis almost an apple.   (I. 5.)

6. Contemplation makes a rare turkey-cock of him. How he jets under his advanced plumes !   (II. 5.)

From *Much Ado about Nothing* :—

7.   For look, where Beatrice, like a lapwing runs,
Close by the ground.   (III. 1.)

From *Midsummer Night's Dream* :—

8.   Brief as the lightning in the collied night,
That in a spleen unfolds both heaven and earth,
And ere a man hath power to say—Behold !
The jaws of darkness do devour it up :
So quick bright things come to confusion.   (I. 1.)

9.   Therefore the moon, the governess of floods,
Pale in her anger, washes all the air,

*   *   *   *   *

And thorough this distemperature we see
The seasons alter.   Hoary-headed frosts
Fall in the fresh lap of the crimson rose ;
And on old Hyem's chin, and icy crown
An odorous chaplet of sweet summer-buds
Is, as in mockery, set.   (II. 2.)

From *The Merchant of Venice* :—

10.   A day in April never came so sweet,
To show how costly summer was at hand,   (II. 9.)

11. And yet, for aught I see, they are as sick that
    surfeit with too much as they that starve with
    nothing.   (I. 2.)

12. Why, this is like the mending of highways
    In summer, where the ways are fair enough. (V. 1.)

From *As You Like It* :—

13.   Wherefore do you follow her
    Like foggy South puffing with wind and rain ?
                                               (III. 5.)
14. Truly the tree yields bad fruit.
    I'll graff it with you ; and then I shall graff it with
    a medlar : then it will be the earliest fruit in the
    country ; for you'll be rotten ere you be half ripe,
    and that's the right virtue of the medlar. (III. 2.)

From *All's Well that Ends Well* :—

15. Your commendations, madam, get from her tears.
    'Tis the best *brine* a maiden can season her praise in.
                                               (I. 1.)
16. We may pick a thousand salads ere we light on such
    another herb.
    Indeed, sir, she was the sweet marjoram of the
    salad, or, rather, the herb of grace.
    They are not salad herbs, you knave.   (IV. 5.)

From 1 *Henry IV.* :—

17. Which makes him prune himself and bristle up
    The crest of youth against your dignity. (I. 1.)

18. For the fortune of us, that are the moon's men, doth
    ebb and flow like the sea, being governed, as the
    sea is, by the moon.   (I. 2.)

19. For, though the camomile, the more it is trodden on
    the faster it grows, yet youth, the more it is
    wasted, the sooner it wears.   (II. 4.)

20. And being fed by us, you us'd us so
    As that ungentle gull, the cuckoo's bird,
    Useth the sparrow : did oppress our nest,
    Grew by our feeding to so great a bulk
    That even our love durst not come near your sight.
                                                       (V. 1.)

From 2 *Henry IV.*:—

21.   (A cause on foot)
    Lives so in hope, as, in an early spring,
    We see the appearing buds : which to prove fruit
    Hope gives not so much warrant, as despair
    That frosts will bite them.   (I. 3.)

22. We shall be winnow'd with so rough a wind
    That even our corn shall seem as light as chaff.
                                                       (IV. 1.)

23. Most subject is the fattest soil to weeds.   (IV. 4.)

From *Henry V.*:—

24. For once the eagle, England, being in prey,
    To her unguarded nest the weasel Scot
    Comes sneaking, and so sucks her princely eggs.
                                                       (I. 2.)

25.   So work the honey-bees,
    Creatures that, by a rule in nature, teach
    The act of order.   (*Idem.*)

From *Troilus and Cressida* :—

26. The nature of the sickness found, Ulysses,
    What is the remedy ?   (I. 3.)

27.   The seeded pride,
    That hath to this maturity blown up
    In rank Achilles, must or now be cropp'd
    Or, shedding, breed a nursery of like evil. (*Idem.*)

From *Coriolanus* :—

28. Of no more soul nor fitness for the world
    Than camels in their war, who have their provand
    Only, for bearing burdens, and sore blows
    For sinking under them.   (II. 1.)

29.   The ripest mulberry
    Now will not hold the handling.   (III. 2.)

From *Julius Cæsar* :—

30. Here lies the East.   Doth not the day break here ?
    No. . . . You shall confess that you are both deceiv'd.
    Here, as I point my sword, the sun arises,
    Which is a great way growing on the south,
    Weighing the youthful season of the year.   (March)
    Some two months hence, up higher toward the
        north
    He first presents his fire.   (II. 1.)

31. But I am constant as the northern star,
    Of whose true-fixed and resting quality
    There is no fellow in the firmament.   (III. 1.)

From *Antony and Cleopatra* :—

32.   They take the flow o' the Nile
By certain scales i' the pyramid. . . .
             The higher Nilus swells
The more it promises. As it ebbs, the seedsman,
Upon the slime and ooze, scatters his grain.
                              (II. 7.)

33. Sometime we see a cloud that's dragonish,
A vapour sometime, like a bear or lion,
A tower'd citadel, a pendent rock,
A forked mountain or blue promontory
With trees upon 't.   (IV. 12.)

From *Cymbeline* :—

34. But you know strange fowl light upon neighbouring
   .ponds.   (I. 5.)

From *King Lear* :—

35. This is the excellent foppery of the world, that
when we are sick in fortune—(often the surfeit of
our own behaviour)—we make guilty of our
disasters the sun, the moon and the stars; as if
we were villains by necessity.   (I. 2.)

36. Oh! how this mother ($\dot{v}\sigma\tau\acute{\epsilon}\rho\alpha$) swells up to my
heart!
Hysterica passio ! Down, thou climbing sorrow;
Thy element's below.   (II. 4.)

37. Winter's not gone yet, if the wild geese fly that way.
                                 (*Idem.*)

38. The art of our necessities is strange
    That can make vile things precious.   (III. 2.)

From *Romeo and Juliet* :—

39. Oh! then I see Queen Mab hath been with you, &c
    (I. 4.)

40.   Here comes Romeo. Without his roe, like a
    dried herring. (II. 4.)

41.   O! mischief, thou art swift
    To enter in the thoughts of desperate men!
    I do remember an apothecary, &c.   (V. 1.)

From *Othello* :—

42. But I will wear my heart upon my sleeve,
    For daws to peck at.   (I. 1.)

43. Our bodies are our gardens, to the which our wills
    are gardeners ;–so that if we will plant nettles or
    sow lettuce . . . . the power and corrigible
    authority of this lies in our wills.   (I. 3.)

44.   My invention
    Comes from my pate, as birdlime does from frize :
    It plucks out brains and all.   (II. 1.)

CHAPTER XX.

AUTHORSHIP OF THE PLAYS, CONTINUED.

Francis Bacon, the Reviser of the Plays, continued—The
Reproduction of his Personal Experience.

BUT we should miss an important proof of
Bacon's work in the Shakespearian drama if we
omitted to point out the reproduction of his
personal experience, which is so remarkable in
some of the pieces. And if he had any hand in
the business, he would scarcely have failed to do
so. His had been no uneventful career. From
first to last it had been out of the ruck of
common men; and, at every period of it, the
words of Diomedes must have occurred to
him :—

Δευκαλίων δ' ἐμὲ τίκτε πολέσσ' ἄνδρεσσιν ἄνακτα.

Deucalion begot me, a king over many men.

Yet fortune seemed determined to treat him

only as a plaything, from those early days, when
he was the youngest and fairest of the great
Queen's courtiers, to that proud but long-
delayed hour when he found himself at the head
of England's tribunals.   But at no time did he
seem to occupy the position he really coveted.
Born in a court, he was not unnaturally fond of
magnificence.   It was a disease he had con-
tracted.   But his heart, like his mind, was
always yearning after knowledge ; and he spoke
no more than its natural language when he said,
in the speech from which we have already
quoted, " that knowledge was the only true and
natural pleasure whereof there was no satiety."
Thus the exertions required for business, or
pleasure, seem to have been like the perfunctory
labours of a wayfaring man, who had turned
aside to tarry but for a night; while the labour
of study was the exercise of affection in the
home where all his joys found rest.   Thus
Dr. Rowley tells us that at sixteen he had
mastered all the learning of his time—a practical
anticipation of the remark that :—

> The spirit of a youth,
> That means to be of note, begins betimes.
>
> (*Antony and Cleopatra*, IV. 4.)

And there can be no doubt he did mean to be
of note. Denied the opportunity of learned
leisure, he applied himself to the study of the
law, which he subsequently (1593) proposed to
reduce to a code ; a work which in 1891 still
remains to be done. At the age of twenty-four
(1585) he entered Parliament as member for
Melcombe, Dorset, and was successively returned
for Taunton (1586), Liverpool (1588), Middlesex
(1592), and Ipswich (1597), while in 1601 he was
returned both for Ipswich and St. Albans, and
in 1614 for Ipswich, St. Albans, and Cambridge.
And from 1588, the year of the Spanish Armada,
he practically led the House of Commons, at
once the advocate of popular rights, and the
supporter of Elizabeth's crown against ambitious
disloyalty and papal intrigue. Philo-papists
professed, and still profess to be horrified by his
pretended ingratitude to the Earl of Essex.
But the ingratitude is a pretence, and nothing
more. He had served the Earl, and his lordship
had insisted on giving him in return a grant of
land, worth not more than sixteen hundred
pounds. But when Bacon consented to accept
it, he did so with the distinct understanding
that it must be with the reservation of his

loyalty to the Queen.* Brutus, therefore, is
answering this Essex scandal when he says :—

If, then, that friend demand why Brutus rose against
Cæsar, this is my answer : Not that I loved Cæsar less, but
that I loved Rome more. Had you rather Cæsar were living
and die all slaves, than that Cæsar were dead to live all
freemen ? . . . . Who is here so vile that will not love his
country ? If any—speak, for him have I offended. I
pause for a reply. (*Julius Cæsar*, III. 2.)

The reply was his double return to the House
of Commons.

But the great Queen had not starved this, the
greatest of her subjects. She probably judged
—and, if she did so, the judgment was right—
that he was not the man to be placed in high
office ; but she had amply provided him with
means for that studious leisure, for which he
was so eminently fit. In 1595 she had made
him her Counsel in the law, and had granted him
one of the crown estates, The Pitts in Zelwood
forest, Somersetshire, with the reversion of the
Registry of the Star Chamber, worth sixteen

* I see I must be your homager and hold land of your gift ; but
do you know the manner of doing homage in law? Always it is
with a saving of his faith to the king and his other lords. (See his
Apology re Essex, Bacon's Works, iii. 215.)

hundred pounds per annum, and of Twickenham
Park and the adjoining lands of Mora Mead and
Ferry Mead.* Those gifts she had supple-
mented three years later, with the rectory of
Cheltenham and King's Charlton, with "all the
land, houses, meadows, pastures, gardens, rents,"
&c., save only the usual rights reserved on
crown lands, and the obligation to maintain two
priests and two deacons, at the nominal rent of
seventy-five pounds, a princely gift if she had
given him nothing else. Before, therefore, he
had attained the age of forty, he was in possession of all a reasonable man would desire, if
only he had been endowed with the smallest
faculty of economic prudence. But that was
the virtue he lacked; and his steward might
have well taken up the words of Flavius, and
said :—

Oh ! my good lord, the world is but a word.
Were it all yours to give it in a breath,
How quickly were it gone ! (*Timon of Athens*, II. 2.)

* It has been constantly asserted that Lord Essex gave Bacon
Twickenham Park; but that was not the piece of land he did give
him. It was not, in fact, his to give; it was crown property, and
had been granted to his kinsman, Edward Bacon, so early as 1574,
and the deed of grant still exists at the Rolls Office (Patent Roll,
16 Eliz., part 6, memb. 3).

S

But the great Queen died, to be succeeded by
the most contemptible, and probably the most
basely vicious sovereign that ever disgraced the
English throne; and from his unworthy hand
came the dangerous honours that proved his
ruin. In 1603 he was knighted; in 1607 he
became solicitor-general; in 1613 attorney-gene-
ral; in 1616 a privy-councillor; in 1617 keeper
of the great seal; in 1618 lord chancellor,
under the title of Baron Verulam, and in 1621
Viscount St. Albans. The same year saw him
" fall, like Lucifer, never to hope again."   .

And during those eighteen years, only three
of which had been spent on the topmost round
of fortune, what had been his life? He had not
been an unjust judge; for not one of his decrees
had been impugned; but, with that exception,
he had been all that a man in high office should
not be. James and his favourite, Buckingham,
had dragged him through the mire of authori-
tative corruption, while his servants not only
squandered the bribes they took in his name,
they joined, with his own love of pomp, in dissi-
pating the vast wealth that was legitimately his
own. That his real pleasures meanwhile consisted in the acquisition of knowledge, and the

preparing of it for distribution, is manifest. If his history of Henry VII. were written to flatter the king, his ' Proficience and Advancement of Learning,' published in 1604, his *De Veterum Sapientia*, published in 1609 and the building up of the new system of philosophy which was destined to enfranchise science, were works worthy of the brightest and wisest of mankind. And like Prospero, he seems to have excused himself by them, for the neglect of his official duties. In fact, Prospero's tale to Miranda is his :—

> Being so reputed
> In dignity and, for the liberal arts,
> Without a parallel, those being all my study,
> The Government I cast upon my brother,
> And to my state grew stranger, transported
> And wrapt in secret studies.   Thy false uncle
> *   *   *   *   ,   *   *
> Being once perfected how to grant suits,
> How to deny them. . . . . . . now he was
> The ivy which had hid my princely trunk
> And sucked my verdure out on't . . . .
> I thus neglecting worldly ends . . he did believe
> He was the duke. . . .
> A treacherous army levied, one midnight,
> Fated to the purpose, did Antonio open
> The gates of Milan . . . and hurried thence.
>
> (*Tempest*, I. 2.)

And, without doubt, Buckingham had been to

Bacon, what Antonio is represented as having been to Prospero. He had practically become the master of the kingdom, and had used the great seal to sanction his unrighteous deeds; and when the people's wrath could be no longer ignored, he, who should have guarded the royal signet, was made the scapegoat. We are not trying to excuse Bacon. Nothing can excuse him. His dereliction of duty was both weak and wicked. We are only noting the story of Prospero as being probably an illustration of the way in which this frail philosopher tried to salve his conscience.

There are many passages in the plays which allude to minor particulars of Bacon's life and connections. Among such we might note that referring to the great bed of *Ware* (*Twelfth Night*, III. 1), "the one whole shirt in Falstaff's company stolen from my trust at *St. Albans*," (1 *Henry IV.*, II. 4), or the assertion of Poins, that Doll Tearsheet was as common as the way between St. Albans and London (2 *Henry IV.*, II. 2), these being as clear allusions to Bacon's county (Hertfordshire) as "Sly of *Burton Heath*," and the fat ale-wife of Wincote (*Induction to Taming the Shrew*), are to Shakespeare's. But a much more significant fact is, that the only attempt to give an exact provincial dialect, has given us the dialect, not of Warwickshire, but of Somersetshire. This is seen in 'King Lear' (IV. 6), when Edgar, who has assumed the character of a peasant, withstands Goneril's steward, and finally kills him ; while Kent, in alluding to *Lipsbury Pinfold* and *Camelot* (II. 2), refers us to the same county. Now Bacon must have known Somersetshire well, while we have no reason to think that Shakespeare did so at all. Then in ' Henry V.' we have Captain Fluellen, whose name is spelt as a Welshman would pronounce Llewhellyn, talking very good Welsh-English ; and we can easily believe he knew Wales from the contiguity of Monmouth to Gloucestershire, where his great estate of Cheltenham Rectory was situated.* Of course it may be said, that perhaps Shakespeare was a great traveller ; but though Aubrey tells us he

---

* His 'Natural History' shows he was acquainted with Wales. Thus he there gives us a piece of Welsh folk-lore as follows— "They say in Wales, when certain hills have their night-caps on they mean mischief" (ix. 819). Now, though Monmouth is now included in England, before the reign of Charles II. it formed part of Wales; and the part adjacent to Gloucestershire is barren and mountainous.

was accustomed to visit Stratford once a year,
we do not hear of any other travelling.   And his
road from London would have been through
Buckinghamshire and Oxfordshire to Warwickshire.   Once, and only once (1605), so far as we
know, did the Globe company go on tour, and
then it was over his accustomed route.   Indeed
the passage in 'Hamlet' would lead us to infer
that travelling was not its custom.   "How
chances it," the Prince asks, "they travel?
Their residence both in reputation and profit was
better both ways." (II. 2.)

But the play which most strikingly illustrates
Bacon's life and recollections is 'Henry VIII.'
It is a complete panorama of his personal expe-
riences.   What a picture it affords of clerical
ambition, and of the indignant protests against
it, which never slumbered!   The speech of
Surrey must have been as familiar in the mouths
of noble lords as household words.

> If we live thus tamely
> To be jaded by a piece of scarlet,
> Farewell nobility.   (III. 2.)

What a life-like presentment of Court manners, too, we have in the scene between Anne

Boleyn and the Court hack, discovering as it does, all the unscrupulous selfishness, the crafty humility, and the sickening hypocrisy of that artful young lady. Well might her companion jeer and say :—

> There was a lady once ('tis an old story)
> Who *would* not be a queen, that would she not,
> For all *the mud in Egypt*. (II. 3.)

But Anne Boleyn is only an allegory. The real subject of the thought is the fascinating pupil of the De Medici, the wife of three husbands, and the murderess of two, the paramour of anybody that will help her to Elizabeth's life and crown, who sits smiling in the castle of Fotheringay, as she thinks of the great Spanish Armada which is to make her a queen and England a land of slaves.

We turn from that to the picture of the dying queen. Of that Dr. Johnson has observed that it—

"Is above any other part of Shakspeare's tragedies, and, perhaps, above any scene of any other poet, tender and pathetick, without gods or furies, or poisons, or precipices, without the help of romantick circumstances, without improbable sallies of poetical lamentation and without any throes of tumultuous misery." (Note to scene II. act 4.)

And certainly, if any one can read it unmoved he never knew what tenderness or pity meant. But of whom was the author thinking?—and it is always some personal recollection that forms the type of an author's happier creations. It could not have been of one he never knew. What was Hecuba to him, or he to Hecuba, that he should weep for her? But the great queen, who had died at Richmond, had found him as a child and befriended him as a man, had given him, in fact, all that was good for him; and no one could have known it better than he. Was he not thinking of her? of her, not discrowned like Catherine, by judicial sentence, but stripped of her dignity by the unfeeling desertion of the court that hurried away to make interest with her successor? Of her who had lain on the ground in a stupor of grief, dying of the ingratitude of those she had loved? Well might his tender heart have conceived that scene, which owes its force to its feeling and to nothing else.

The rapid march of events and the momentous changes that took place during the interim, give us the idea that a long period separates Lord St. Albans from Cardinal Wolsey. But when Bacon was disgraced (1621), less than a century had passed since the fall of Wolsey, (1529); and though no one may have been alive who knew the arrogant churchman personally, his story must have been fresh in men's minds. How much it resembled Bacon's could have been known to no one better than to Bacon himself. Both had been profuse, ostentatious and ambitious; both had held the same high office in the state, and both had been suddenly cast out of it. There was perhaps but little similarity in their inner characters, but in their ruin they were one; and, when it came, each could have said :—

I have touched the highest point of all my greatness;
And, from that full meridian of my glory,
I haste now to my setting. I shall fall
Like a bright exhalation in the evening,
And no man see me more.

But the reproach of kings comes with far better grace from the philosopher than the priest. The latter had tried to make the king an instrument in elevating him above all kings; the former had been only too subservient to his lawful sovereign, and might justly complain :—

. . . . O, how wretched
Is that poor man that hangs on princes' favours !
There is betwixt the smile we would aspire to,
The sweet aspect of princes, and their ruin
More pangs and fears than wars or women have ;
And when he falls, he falls like Lucifer,
Never to hope again.   (III. 2.)

Again, when Griffiths, having craved permission to recount the good of the Lord Cardinal, reminds the queen of " the twins of learning " he had raised, we seem to hear Bacon reminding posterity of what he had done for it.   And, during his last years, that thought was never absent from his mind.   We see it in his fable of the ' New Atlantis,' which anticipates the mighty revolution in knowledge he had inaugurated ; we read it in the dying bequest of his character to future generations, which, as he surely foresaw, have crowned his memory with immortal praise.

From these, therefore, and like considerations, we conclude that ' Henry VIII.' also was his entire composition.   It not only embodies much of his experience, it is written in his style from beginning to end ; whether we regard the pageantry of which he was so fond, the characterization in which he was such an adept, or the bantering humour for which he was so re-markable.

In concluding our notice of the revision we must not omit to point out its inequality in different pieces. Some have apparently been al-most re-written ; such as ' King Lear,' ' Macbeth,' ' Merchant of Venice,' ' The Tempest,' the two parts of ' Henry IV.,' ' Much Ado about Nothing,' ' As you like it ' and ' Twelfth Night.' Others have only been touched here and there ; such as ' Othello,' ' Romeo and Juliet,' and ' A Mid-summer Night's Dream ' ; while a few show no signs of revision. These are, first, ' Titus An-dronicus,' ' Love's Labour's Lost,' ' 1 Henry VI.,' and the ' Comedy of Errors ; ' and second, ' Julius Cæsar,' ' Antony and Cleopatra,' ' Corio-lanus,' and '·Timon of Athens.' Those in the first category exhibit none of the embroidery of which Malone speaks. They are composed entirely of the coarse stuff originally made up for the stage. They never, perhaps, achieved any popularity, and were not, therefore, con-sidered worth the expense of revision. Those in the second category, though not remarkable for dramatic excellence, are exclusively composed of fine cloth. They, therefore, were probably composed, in the first instance, by Francis Bacon.

We do not,[1] like Malone, found an argument for revision on the difference between the quarto and folio editions. It had begun, we think, before Robert Greene died (1592), which would be two years before the first quarto appeared (2 Henry VI., 1594). That there was a general over-hauling for the first folio (1623), may be likely enough ; but, if so, it would only be the last act in the revision.

CHAPTER XXI.

SHAKESPEARE'S POEMS.

Sonnets by Anthony and Francis Bacon and their Friends.

THERE is no doubt that the contemporaries of William Shakespeare recognized him as the author of 'Venus and Adonis' and of the 'Rape of Lucrece;' but the Sonnets stand in another category. No one, except Francis Meres, ascribes them to him; but it is evident he means us to take Shakespeare as their actual composer. His words, indeed, can admit of no other interpretation.

"As the soul of Euphorbus was thought to live in Pythagoras," he says, "so the sweet, witty soul of Ovid lives in mellifluous, honey-tongued Shakespeare. Witness his 'Venus and Adonis,' his 'Lucrece,' his sugared sonnets *among his friends.*" (*Palladis Tamia*, 1598.)

Now the 'Sonnets' were first published in 1609. It is, therefore, obvious that William Shakespeare had handed them, or, rather some of them, about among his friends, as his own composition, eleven years, at least, but perhaps more, before they were printed. Meres, of course, took his word for them, as he had done for the plays. But when the 'Sonnets' are printed they are not printed by Shakespeare, nor are they described as his composition. On the contrary, they are declared to be the work of somebody else. To save readers the trouble of turning back to Chapter XI. we again transcribe their title-page.

SHAKSPEARE'S SONNETS

NEVER BEFORE IMPRINTED

AT LONDON BY GELD FOR T.T. AND ARE TO
BE SOLD BY WILLIAM ASPLEY
1609. 4to.

And T. T. prefixes the following ascription to them :—

To The

ONLY BEGETTER OF THESE ENSUING SONNETS,

Mr. W. H.

ALL HAPPINESS AND THAT ETERNITY PROMISED BY OUR
EVER-LIVING POET   WISHETH THE WELL-WISHING
ADVENTURER IN SETTING FORTH.
T. T.

And what is the natural interpretation of this remarkable announcement? Is it not that the 'Sonnets,' formerly ascribed to Shakespeare, are the sole product of Mr. W. H., whoever that may be? If not, what interpretation can be given? Mr. W. H. is not the printer. Geld prints them. He is not the publisher. William Aspley publishes them. He is not the person, who causes them to be published and is responsible for the undertaking. T. T. is that adventurer. Unless he be the author, he has no connection with them; and the reference to him is impertinent.

The description of him, "the only begetter of these ensuing sonnets," may, however, imply more than actual composer. It seems to suggest that he wrote some of them himself and was the cause of others being written by different persons. And that is the proposition we shall deduce from their internal evidence; for it is obvious they were not all written by the same individual.

But who is Mr. W. H? It has been argued that, as the sonnets reveal the same mind as the plays, they were written by the same author. And many of them do display a similar mind.

We, therefore, on that argument, might ascribe them to Francis Bacon. But we shall prefer to attribute them to his brother Anthony, and other of his friends, on the strength of their own internal evidence.

Thus, taking the first thirty-two sonnets, we see at a glance they were the composition of two different persons, both men, tenderly attached to each other, the one, who begins, dying first. He, as we conceive, wrote from I. to XXXI. and left XXXII. unfinished. Like other sonnets of the time they were imitations of Petrarch, and display but little poetic talent. They are addressed to him, who finishes No. XXXII. No. XXXII. commences as follows :—

XXXII.

If thou survive my well contented day,
    When that churl, death, my bones with dust shall cover,
And shall by fortune once more resurvey
    These poor, rude lines of thy deceased lover,
Compare them with the bettering of the time,
    And though they be outstripp'd by every pen,
Reserve them for my love, not for their rhyme,
    Exceeded by the height of happier men.
Oh! then vouchsafe me but this loving thought.

But here he becomes silent, and the second adds—

Had my friend's muse grown with this growing age,
A dearer birth than this his love had brought,
To march in ranks of better equipage.
But since *he died* and poets better prove,
Theirs for their style I'll read ; his for his love.

How exactly this applies to the two brothers !
They were remarkable for brotherly love at a
time, when family affection had not yet been
laughed out of countenance, insomuch that
though Anthony had an estate and Francis none,
there was a common purse between them.   Then
Anthony died in 1601 ; while Francis survived
till 1626.

But the intermediate sonnets furnish addi-
tional illustrations of their experience.   XXII.
tells us. the writer was older than he whom he
addressed ; and. Anthony was the senior by two
years ; XXVI. and XXVII. that the writer was
living at a distance ; and Anthony was in
France, Navarre, and Venice during the time
Francis was keeping his terms at Gray's Inn ;
while XX. says :—

XX.

A woman's face, with Nature's own hand painted,
    Hast thou, the master-mistress of my passion,
A woman's gentle heart, but not acquainted
    With shifting change, as is false woman's fashion.

T

And the habits, as well as the youthful appearance of Bacon, were more suited to a refined girl in our days than to a man in his. Witness his love of flowers, of perfumes and fine clothes, and his constant use of hot baths at a period when folks scarcely washed their faces.

Then, though the burden of the earlier sonnets was copied from Petrarch, Anthony was really grieved at the thought that his brother, of whom he was so proud, was allowing youth to slip away without providing any successor, and might therefore naturally remind him that :—

II.

When forty winters shall besiege thy brow,
And dig deep trenches in thy beauty's field,
Thy youth's proud livery, so gazed on now,
Will be a tatter'd weed of small worth held.

But Francis, absorbed in dreams of ambition, seemed to have been always repeating to himself his own maxim: "He that hath wife and children hath given hostages to fortune." And so, when at last he does marry, he has turned forty-six.

We assert, therefore, with much confidence, that Anthony wrote the first thirty-one sonnets and part of the thirty-second. The remainder, which brings up the total number of poems to a hundred and fifty-four, was not, we think, entirely the work of Francis. Those addressed to a youth display none of his characteristics, but are evidently of female inspiration; and, considering his personal attractions and the notoriously amorous character of the queen's court-ladies, we can easily imagine he had many admirers within their circle. With those exceptions, he wrote, we think, all the rest. They reveal not only his style but his story. What could have described his first disappointment more forcibly than that with which he commences :—

XXXIII.

Full many a glorious morning have I seen
    Flatter the mountain-tops with sovereign eye,
Kissing with golden face the meadows green,
    Gilding pale streams with heavenly alchemy,
    Anon permit the basest clouds to ride
With ugly rack on his celestial face,
    And from the forlorn world his visage hide,
Stealing unseen to West with this disgrace.
    E'en so my sun one early morn did shine
With all triumphant glory on my brow ;
    But, out, alack ! he was but one hour mine,
The region cloud hath mask'd him from me now.

T 2

Yet him for this my love no whit disdaineth.
Suns of the world may stain when heaven's sun staineth.

In this we seem to be reading of the year 1593,
when he was denied his first step to the wool-
sack—the post of solicitor-general—and can
fancy we see him retiring in deep dejection from
court with nothing but a mournful recollection
of those happy early days when the Queen used
to pat his fair cheek, and call him her " young
lord-keeper."

Some, the reader will observe, abound in legal
terms ; as—

XLVI.

Mine eye and heart are at a mortal war
   How to divide the conquest of thy sight,
Mine eye my heart thy picture's sight would bar
   My heart mine eye the freedom of that right.
My heart doth plead that thou in him dost lie,
   A closet never pierced by crystal eyes ;
But the defendant doth that plea deny,
   And says in him thy fair appearance lies.
To 'cide this title is impannellèd
   A quest of thoughts, all tenants to the heart ;
And by their verdict is determinèd
     The clear eye's moiety and the dear heart's part.
   And my heart's right thy inward love of heart.

Others reproduce ideas found in Bacon's
acknowledged works ; as—

LIX.

If there be nothing new, but that which is
   Hath been before, how are our brains beguiled,
Which, labouring for invention, bear amiss
   The second burden of a former child !

A sentiment which finds a parallel in essay No. 58 ; viz.,

Plato had an imagination that knowledge was but memory ; and Solomon giveth his sentence that novelty is oblivion.

The love-sonnets written by Bacon, easily distinguishable from those written by women to him, are not, we think, all addressed to one person. Some may have been devoted to Lady Hatton, during his suit to her; but his wife Alice must certainly be the object of those which culminate in CLII. To none else could the last be applicable :—

CLII.

In loving thee thou know'st I am forsworn ;
   But thou art twice forsworn to me love swearing ;
In act thy bed-vow broke and new faith torn,
   In vowing new hate after new love bearing.

Nos. CLIII. and CLIV., the latter merely a

paraphrase of the former, appear to be the commencement of a new series that was carried no farther.

It is, of course, superfluous to point out that nothing in these sonnets bears any affinity to the vulgar, uneducated player of the Blackfriars and Globe theatres.

CHAPTER XXII.

SHAKESPEARE'S POEMS.

The 'Venus and Adonis' and 'Rape of Lucrece,' by Marlowe.

THOUGH Shakespeare openly published 'Venus and Adonis' and the 'Rape of Lucrece' as his own works, and, though impugning the fact charges him with being an absolute impostor, we shall impugne it nevertheless. Both those poems are manifestly beyond him who wrote the epitaphs on Coombe and Ben Jonson. They are the composition of an educated, if not of a refined mind, and of an author who was imbued with the true poetic spirit.

Venus and Adonis is suggested by Ovid's story in the Metamorphoses (x. xii. to xv.); but there is no such servile following of its original as would have been adopted by a novice, who was reading it for the first time in a translation. On the contrary, the author strikes out from it with a boldness only to be expected from an intimate familiarity with the original. This, however, is only a preliminary objection to Shakespeare's claim; our strong point is that internal evidence shows it was the work of Christopher Marlowe.

It is written exactly in the style of his 'Hero and Leander,' and exhibits such similarities to it as might be expected in two works written by the same author on a cognate subject. Both are offensively lascivious, both rich in poetic imagery, both overpowering by their impetuosity; so that they enchain the attention in spite of the reader's better judgment. And we have abundant evidence that 'Venus and Adonis' created quite a sensation among the reading public when it first appeared. Grave censors, indeed, were chary of their praise; and Gabriel Harvey represents their judgment when he says :—

The *younger sort* take much delight in Shakspeare's Venus and Adonis, but his Lucrece and his tragedy of Hamlet, prince of Denmark, have it in them to please the wiser sort.

But everybody read it; women, we are told, reading it on the sly.

And the reproduction of ideas is not from Hero and Leander' to 'Venus and Adonis,' but from 'Venus and Adonis' to 'Hero and Leander;' and if our hypothesis be correct, the former was in MS. complete before Marlowe began to write the latter. And that he had not given up the intention of publishing 'Venus and Adonis' when he commenced 'Hero and Leander' is evident; because he plainly refers to it in his description of Hero's dress :—

> Her wide sleeves green and bordered with a grove,
> Where Venus, in her naked glory strove
> . To please the careless and disdainful eyes
> Of proud Adonis, that before her lies. (*Ses.* I. 11, &c.)

And whence, otherwise does he get "the careless and disdainful eyes" of Adonis? The idea of the youth's reluctance is propounded, *for the first time*, in 'Venus and Adonis.' Musæus suggests nothing of the sort; indeed, his only reference to Adonis is that the people had flocked to Sestos, where the festival to Venus and Adonis was being celebrated :—

> δὴ γὰρ κυπρίδιη πανδήμος ἦλθεν ἑορτή,
> τὴν ἀνὰ Σηστὸν ἄγουσιν Ἀδώνιδι καὶ Κυθερείῃ.
> (*Il. & L.* 42–3.)

And, so far from being suggested by Ovid,
the idea that he was too young for love, when
Venus and he retire into the grove, contradicts
what he does say of him :—

Jam *vir*, jam se formosior ipso est,
Jam placet Veneri.   (X. xi. 5, 6.)

Neither is there anything in the ancient fables
which lends even a colour to the suggestion.
Adonis was merely a symbol of the sun, the
most active of all natural agents—a power that
vivified all animate things, from the αὐτόχθονες
to the ἔντομι. Unless, therefore, we can believe
that Marlowe had so little desire to be understood, that he referred to an idea which was
confined to his own mind, we must believe he
referred to a poem he intended to publish before
he made ' Hero and Leander' public.

But there are many ideas which, having no
type in Musæus, find parallels in ' Venus and
Adonis ; ' and to some of them we now beg the
reader's attention, asking him, at the same time,
to observe the similarity in the poetry which
clothes them.

Thus, the description of Hero's beauty repeats
the idea used in describing that of Adonis :—

So lovely fair was Hero, Venus' nun,
As nature wept, thinking she was undone ;
Because she took more from her than she left,
And of such wondrous beauty her bereft.
Therefore, in sign her treasure suffered wrack,
Since Hero's time hath half the world been black.

(H. & L., I.)

And in ' Venus and Adonis ' we read :—

" Thrice fairer than myself," thus she began,
" The field's chief flower, sweet beyond compare,
Stain to all nymphs, more lovely than a man,
More white and red than doves and roses are.
Nature, that made thee, with herself at strife,
Saith that the world hath ending with thy life.

(V. & A., II.)

Then the effect of amorous glances is similarly
repeated, when we are told that—

By this sad Hero, with love unacquainted,
Viewing Leander's face, fell down and fainted.
He kissed her and breathed life into her lips.

(H. & L., II.)

While in ' Venus and Adonis ' we read :—

And at his look she falleth flatly down ;
For looks kill love, and love by looks reviveth.

*   *   *   *

The silly boy, believing she is dead,

Claps her pale cheek, till clapping makes it red

   *   *   *   *

For on the grass she lies, as she were slain,
Till his breath breatheth life in her again.

                          (*V. & A.* 78.)

So, also, beauty's obligations to love impressed on Leander is impressed on Adonis in much the same terms.

> And such, as knew he was a man would say,
> " Leander, thou art made for amorous play.
> Why art thou not in love and loved of all ?
> *Though thou be fair, yet be not thine own thrall."*
>
>   (*H. & L.,* I.)

And in ' Venus and Adonis '—

> " The tender Spring, upon thy tempting lip,
> Shews thee unripe, yet may'st thou well be tasted.
> Make use of time, let not advantage slip,
> *Beauty within itself should not be wasted."*
>
>   (*V. & A.* 22.)

But another fact obtrudes itself on our attention. It is evident that the first stanza of our version of 'Venus and Adonis' could not originally have been the commencement of the poem, because it lands us at once *in medias res.*

Even as the sun, with purple-coloured face,
　Had ta'en his last leave of the weeping morn,
Rose-cheeked Adonis hied him to the chase.
　Hunting he loved, but love he laughed to scorn.
Sick-thoughted Venus makes amain unto him
And like a bold-faced suitor, 'gins to woo him.

We have not been told who Adonis is; we
have no idea why Venus approaches him, nor
the slightest conception why she is sick-
thoughted when doing so. Something has
obviously been omitted which would have ex-
plained all. Ovid's story has no such deficiencies.
His account, contained in the 10th, 11th, 12th,
13th, and 14th fables of the 10th book of ' The
Metamorphoses,' is perfectly explicit and satis-
factory. The 10th fable narrates the birth of
Adonis and the transformation of his mother
Myrrha into the myrrh-tree; the 11th his
education by the Naïads, his beauty, and the
passion which leads Venus to forsake Olympus
and accompany him in his hunting expeditions;
the 12th how, after the chase, she invites him
into a poplar grove, where they recline on the
grass, as she speaks of the danger of pursuing
bears and lions. In the 13th she relates to him
the story of Atalanta and Hippomanis; and in

the 14th we have the account of his death and
transformation into the anemone. We may,
therefore, confidently assert that, at least, several
stanzas are wanting. And, if that be so, we
need no better proof to convince us that ' Venus
and Adonis ' was not published by its author.

But there is evidence that it was sub-
mitted to revisions before it was printed. Thus
the stanza beginning "Bid me discourse," and
that which follows it, constitute a transparent
interpolation. They harmonise neither with
what precedes them nor what follows them.
Thus Venus had been saying—

> Thou canst not see one wrinkle in my brow;
>   My eyes are gray and bright and quick in turning;
> My beauty, as the Spring, doth yearly grow;
>   My flesh is plump, my marrow burning;
> My smooth, moist hand, were it with thy hand felt,
> Would in thy palm dissolve or seem to melt.
>
> (*V. & A.* 24.)

This surely is the prelude to an invitation
very different to—

> Bid me discourse, I will enchant thine ear,
>   Or, like a fairy, trip upon the green;
> Or, like a nymph, with bright disheveled hair,
>   Dance on the sands and yet no footing seen.
> Love is a spirit all compact of fire,
> Not gross to sink, but light and will aspire. (*V. & A.* 25.)

If love be such a spirit, the allusion to "plump flesh" and "burning marrow" was a grand mistake on the part of Mdme. Venus. But no one, we think, can doubt that something too gross, even for that age, was expunged, and that these inconsequential verses were inserted in its place.

The Rape of Lucrece is also in Marlowe's style, though it, too, has manifestly undergone revision; but having, as we think, proved our case in regard to 'Venus and Adonis,' we may assign 'Lucrece' to Marlowe on the sole ground of similarity in style.

We do not feel called upon to prove the precise manner in which Shakespeare became possessed of the MSS. of these two poems. He was the friend (heaven save the mark!) of the unfortunate author, and would probably have had access to his lodgings after his decease. Once there, he might have over-hauled his papers and taken what he fancied.

The other poems, which go under Shakespeare's name, may have been written by any second-rate poet of the time; but, as the worst of them does not sink to a level with the epitaph on John Coombe, we decline to believe that any of them were written by William Shakespeare.

CHAPTER XXIII.

CONCLUSION.

THE issue raised and argued in the foregoing pages is the origin of those works, plays, and poems which go under the name of Shakespeare; an issue which, so far as the plays are concerned, divides itself into two branches :—

I. Arc they original compositions ?

II. Who were, or was the authors or author ?

In endeavouring to answer these questions we have shown—

1. That English literature, when the plays appeared, was extensively tinctured with classical learning (Chap. I.).

2. That the drama, which had just come into fashion, was formed on classical models (Chap. II.).

3. That the characteristics of the plays show they were written by learned men (Chap. III.).

4. That so far, however, from being original, their originals are to be found, respectively, in

the Greek, Roman, Spanish and Italian drama (Chaps. IV., V., VI., VII.).

5. That the incidence of their publication does not reveal the author (Chap. XI.).

6. That William Shakespeare's literary character, as gathered from contemporary opinion, was not such as became the author of the plays (Chaps. XII. and XIII.).

7. That his personal character was consistent with that of a literary impostor, whose wealth . had enabled him to make use of needy scholars . (Chap. XIV.).

8. That such scholars were numerous and their necessities pressing (Chaps. I. and XV.).

9. That, in fact, more than six such scholars employed by him to write plays were named or referred to by a contemporary in 1592 (Chaps. XV., XVI., XVII.).

10. That another contemporary asserted in 1589 that the author of 'Hamlet' was a lawyer ; and that while Shakespeare was none, Francis Bacon was a poet of distinguished learning and genius, and the only lawyer of the time likely to engage in such an employment, as he was the only one capable of writing 'Hamlet' (Chap. XVIII.) ·

11. And that Robert Greene, Christopher

Marlowe, Thomas Nash, George Peele, Samuel
Daniel, Thomas Lodge, George Chapman, and
Francis Bacon were respectively the authors of
'Love's Labour's Lost,' and the 'Comedy of
Errors,' the second and third parts of 'Henry
VI.,' and 'Richard III.', 'The Winter's Tale,' 'A
Midsummer Night's Dream,' 'Romeo and Juliet,'
'Love's Labour Won (As You Like It),' 'Mac-
beth' and 'The Tempest,' and 'Hamlet' (Chaps.
XV., XVI., XVII., and XVIII.).

12. That, in consequence of the great favour
with which 'Hamlet' was received in or before
1589, Shakespeare engaged Francis Bacon, under
a promise of secrecy, to revise the plays he had
obtained or should obtain from other authors;
and that Robert Greene and others ascribed the
revision to Shakespeare himself, and therefore
taunted him with pretending he could "bombast
out a blank verse as well as the best of them"
(Chaps. XIX., and XV.).

13. That as Bacon's composition of 'Hamlet'
is proved by the parallel passages found in his
acknowledged works (Chap. XVIII.); so his
revision of the other plays—excepting always
'Titus Andronicus,' 'Love's Labour's Lost,' and
the 'Comedy of Errors'—is proved not only by

parallel passages, but by the presence of his tone of thought, mode of illustration and personal experience; and that 'Julius Cæsar,' 'Antony and Cleopatra,' ' Coriolanus,' 'Timon of Athens,' and ',Henry VIII.' were also his entire composition (Chaps. XIX. and XX.).

14. That the best pieces in the series are reproductions of more archaic plays ; but that, so far as English beauties are concerned, Francis Bacon, with some assistance from Samuel Daniel, is the genius of Shakespeare.

15. The 'Sonnets of Shakespeare,' we find to be the production of Anthony and Francis Bacon and some of the friends of Francis (Chap. XXI.), and 'Venus and Adonis,' and 'The Rape of Lucrece,' of Christopher Marlowe.

APPENDIX.

No. I.—THE PLAYS, WITH THEIR ORIGINALS AND ENGLISH AUTHORS, PROVED OR PROBABLE.

Dates	Plays	Originals	English Original Authors
Before 1589	Love's Labour's Lost (G. of Wit)	.	Robert Greene
„	Comedy of Errors	{Menœchmi and Amphitryo} (Plautus)	Robert Greene
„	Winter's Tale	Andria (Terence)	Robert Greene and Thomas Nash
„	Midsummer Night's Dream	Italian Drama	George Peele and Drayton
„	Richard III.	Hall	Christopher Marlowe
„	Henry VI., 2 and 3	.	Francis Bacon
„	Hamlet	Electra (Sophocles)	„
1592	Romeo and Juliet (Menaphon)	Spanish Drama (Lopez de Vega)	Samuel Daniel
„	{Love's Labour Won (As You Like It)}	.	Thomas Lodge
1594	Taming the Shrew (On Register)	.	{Samuel Daniel or Michael Drayton?
1598	Richard II.	.	{Samuel Daniel or Michael Drayton
„	Henry IV., 1 and 2	Hollinshed	Unknown
„	King John	„	„
„	Two Gentlemen of Verona	.	
„	Merchant of Venice	Spanish Drama	George Peele ?
„	Titus Andronicus	.	Unknown

1600	Much Ado about Nothing	Spanish Drama	„
„	Henry V.	Hollinshed	„
1602	Merry Wives of Windsor	Henry IV., 1 and 2	„
1604	Othello.	Spanish Drama	Christopher Marlowe?
1608	King Lear	Geoffrey of Monmouth	Unknown
1609	Troilus and Cressida	The Iliad	„
1623	Macbeth	Agamemnon (Æschylus)	George Chapman
„	The Tempest	Rudens (Plautus)	„
„	Anthony and Cleopatra	Plutarch's Lives	Francis Bacon
„	Julius Cæsar	„	„
„	Coriolanus	„	„
„	Timon of Athens	„	„
„	Henry VIII.	Hollinshed	„
„	All's Well that Ends Well		„
„	Cymbeline	Livy	Unknown
„	Measure for Measure		„
„	Twelfth Night	Gli Inganni	„
„	Henry VI, 1	Hall	„

N.B.—The dates are of course only approximate. 'Hamlet' must have been produced before 1589 (see Nash's 'Preface to Menaphon'), and we have assumed that his bitterness was occasioned by the appearance as a dramatist of the young lawyer who was thus supplanting him and his friends (Greene, Marlowe, and Peele) in Shakespeare's theatre. If that hypothesis be correct, their plays, to which Greene referred in 1592 (Groatsworth of Wit), must have been written before 'Hamlet' appeared. So, if the "two more" he mentions were Samuel Daniel and Thomas Lodge, and they were the authors of 'Romeo and Juliet' and 'As You Like It,' their plays must have been written before he died (1592). Then 'Henry V.' and 'Much Ado about Nothing' were printed in 4to. edition in 1600, and 'Othello' was represented at the court revels in 1604; while the 'Merry Wives of Windsor,' 'King Lear,' and 'Troilus and Cressida' were respectively published in 4to. editions in 1602, 1608, and 1609, and 'Taming the Shrew' was entered on the Stationers' Register in 1594.

No. II.—THE VARIOUS EARLY PUBLICATIONS OF SHAKESPEARE'S PLAYS.

PUBLISHED IN 4TO WITH SHAKESPEARE'S NAME.

1. Love's Labour's Lost 1598
2. Midsummer Night's Dream . . . 1600
3. Merchant of Venice . . . . —
4. Henry IV., 2 . . . . . —
5. Much Ado about Nothing . . . —
6. Merry Wives of Windsor . . . 1602
7. Hamlet 1603
8. Troilus and Cressida 1609
9. King John 1611
10. Pericles of Tyre . . . . . —
11. Othello 1622

PUBLISHED IN 4TO WITHOUT SHAKESPEARE'S NAME.

1. Henry VI., 2 1594
2. Henry VI., 3 1595
3. Richard II. 1597
4. Richard III. . . . . . —
5. Romeo and Juliet . . . . —
6. Henry IV., 1 1598
7. Titus Andronicus 1600
8. Henry V. . . . . . . —
9. King Lear 1608

FIRST PUBLISHED IN THE FOLIO OF 1623.

1. Antony and Cleopatra.
2. All's Well that Ends Well.
3. As You Like It.
4. Cymbeline.
5. Coriolanus.
6. Comedy of Errors.
7. Henry VIII.
8. Julius Cæsar.
9. Macbeth.
10. Measure for Measure.
11. Tempest.

12. Timon of Athens.
13. Taming the Shrew.
14. Twelfth Night.
15. Two Gentlemen of Verona.
16. Winter's Tale.
17. Henry VI., 1

N.B.—Pericles of Tyre was omitted.

OTHER PLAYS PUBLISHED WITH SHAKESPEARE'S NAME.

Written by.

1. Arthur of Faversham	1592	4to.			
2. Locrine	1595	,,			
3. Edward III.	1596	,,			
4. Sir John Oldcastle	1600	,,	fo. 1663	Anth. Munday	
5. Thomas Ld. Cromwell	1602	,,	,,	,,	
6. London Prodigal	1605	,,	,,	,,	
7. Puritan Widow	1607	,,	,,	,,	
8. Yorkshire Tragedy	1608	,,	,,	,,	
9. Pericles of Tyre	1609	,,	,,	,,	
10. Two Noble Kinsmen	1634	,,			
11. Birth of Merlin	1662	,,			
12. Lord Cobham			fo. 1663		

No. III.—LIST OF PLAYS AND PLAYERS PREFIXED
TO THE FOLIO EDITION OF 1623.

A CATALOGUE OF THE SEVERAL COMEDIES, HISTORIES,
AND TRAGEDIES CONTAINED IN THIS VOLUME.

COMEDIES.

Tempest.
Two Gentlemen of Verona.
Merry Wives of Windsor.
Measure for Measure.
The Comedy of Errors.
Much Ado about Nothing.
Love's Labour's Lost.
Midsummer Night's Dream.
Merchant of Venice.

As You Like it.
Taming of the Shrew.
All's Well that Ends Well.
Twelfth Night, or What You Will.
Winter's Tale.

HISTORIES.

The Life and Death of King John.
The Life and Death of King Richard the Second.
The First Part of King Henry the Fourth.
The Second Part of King Kenry the Fourth.
The Life of King Henry the Fifth.
The First Part of King Henry the Sixth.
The Second Part of King Henry the Sixth.
The Third Part of King Henry the Sixth.
The Life and Death of King Richard the Third.
The Life of Henry the Eighth.

TRAGEDIES.

The Tragedy of Coriolanus.
Titus Andronicus.
Romeo and Juliet.
Timon of Athens.
The Life and Death of Julius Cæsar.
The Tragedy of Macbeth.
The Tragedy of Hamlet.
King Lear.
Othello, the Moor of Venice.
Antony and Cleopatra.
Cymbeline, King of Britain.

N.B.—Though 'Troilus and Cressida' is not in this list, it is included in the book, and stands as the first of the tragedies.

THE NAMES OF THE PRINCIPAL ACTORS IN ALL THESE PLAYS.

William Shakespeare	Samuel Gilburne
Richard Burbage	Robert Armin
John Hemmings	William Ostler

Augustine Phillips
William Kempt
Thomas Poope
George Bryan
Henry Condell
William Slye
Richard Cowley
John Lowine
Samuel Crosse
Alexander Cooke

Nathan Field
John Underwood
Nicholas Tooley
William Eccleston
Joseph Taylor
Robert Benfield
Robert Ganghe
Richard Robinson
John Shancke
John Rice

No. IV.—FRANCIS MERES' LIST OF SHAKESPEARE'S PLAYS IN 1598, FROM THE 'PALLADIS TAMIA,' 1598 (C. of P., p. 21).

1. Richard II.
2. Richard III.
3. Henry IV.
4. King John.
5. Titus Andronicus.
6. Romeo and Juliet.
7. Comedy of Errors.
8. Love's Labour's Lost.
9. Love's Labour Won (As You Like It?).
10. Two Gentlemen of Verona.
11. Midsummer Night's Dream.
12. Merchant of Venice.
13. Hamlet.
14. Henry VI.

LONDON:
PRINTED BY WILLIAM CLOWES AND SONS, LIMITED,
STAMFORD STREET AND CHARING CROSS.